GIRLS CAN'T BE PILOTS

Aim High.

Margaret Ringenberg

GIRLS CAN'T BE PILOTS

An Aerobiography

Margaret J. Ringenberg
with Jane L. Roth

*Daedalus Press * Fort Wayne, Indiana*

Published by Daedalus Press
Box 8962, Fort Wayne, Indiana 46898-8962

Manufactured in the United States of America

Cover design by
Carolyn Utesch
Courier Printing, Grabill, Indiana

Publisher's Cataloging-in-Publication
(Provided by Quality Books, Inc.)

Ringenberg, Margaret J.
    Girls can't be pilots: an aerobiography by
Margaret J.Ringenberg with Jane L. Roth. -- 1st ed.
    p. cm.
Includes bibliographical references and index.
Preassigned LCCN: 98-70166
ISBN: 0-9661859-0-0

    1. Ringenberg, Margaret J. 2. Women air pilots--
United States--Biography. 3. Women's Air Service
Pilots (U.S.)
I. Roth, Jane L. II Title.

TL540.R56 1998   629.13'092
                                  QBI198-290

10 9 8 7 6 5 4 3 2
First Edition

Dedication

To my folks, Albert and Lottie Ray, for letting me do my own thing.

To my husband, Morris Ringenberg, and my children, Marsha Ringenberg Wright and Mike Ringenberg, for granting me time away from home to pursue my passion.

To my son-in-law, Steve Wright who thinks I'm "one tough mother-in-law."

To my grandchildren, Jonathan, Joseph, Joshua, Jairus, and Jaala, who, when they were little, would look up whenever an airplane passed over and say, "There goes Grandma!"

And to my students and passengers who were brave enough to ride with a "girl" pilot.
MJR

To my mother who gave me life.
To my children who are my life.
JLR

5

CONTENTS

Photo sections follow Parts Two and Four

Acknowledgments

We have not attempted to cite in the text, all the sources consulted in the preparation of this book. To do so would require more space than is available. The list would include government publications, libraries, periodicals, and many individuals. Let me thank those who helped in the writing and publication of this book: Dorothy Morse who read the first draft, Larry Mack whose services as proofreader/editor were invaluable, Marsha Wright who helped immensely with interviewing, editing, and encouragement, Shell Semler for acquiring software, Christine White, Kathy King, and the people at Bookcrafters for sharing their expertise, Carolyn Utesch and the people at Courier Printing for the cover and pictures.

Information has been contributed by: Senator Dan Coats, Fred Bunyan, Mary Thompson, Marsha Wright, Steve Wright, Tony Niewyck, Marty Wyall, Pat Keefer, Rev. Mike Livingston, Lois Feigenbaum, Bruce Bone, Morris Ringenberg, and Mike Ringenberg. I sincerely thank these people for the part they played in telling this story.

JLR

"Let her swim, climb mountain peaks, pilot airplanes, battle against the elements, take risks, go out for adventure, and she will not feel before the world. . .timidity." Simone de Beauvoir

Foreword

I have flown with Margaret Ringenberg many times, often on very short notice. One of my more memorable experiences was campaigning with Dan Quayle during the 1988 Presidential campaign. Leaving Washington very early in the morning under the protection of the Secret Service, we traveled by limo to Dulles Airport to board the large 727 specially outfitted for the Vice President and his staff, Secret Service, the Press and other guests. It was equipped to serve a full breakfast and snacks, offered newspapers from major cities, and contained a fax, copy machine, typewriters, special communication equipment and secretaries—all the trimmings.

After several other stops, we landed in Columbus, Ohio. I needed to get to Fort Wayne, Indiana, for campaign appearances of my own, but there were no scheduled flights from Columbus to Fort Wayne. Margaret came to the rescue, arriving in a little Cessna, which looked very small alongside the Vice President's "Hoosier Pride." It was quite a contrast when I transferred from the private 727 to a rented Cessna with barely enough room for luggage and my long legs.

Now, I'll let you in on a little secret: I don't

really enjoy flying. I'm one of those nervous fliers who sweats out every little bump. But a funny thing happens when I fly with Margaret. I don't worry about a thing. I just have complete trust in her. Normally my staff has a rule about my flying — two pilots, two engines, and FAA certified flying service. We don't make exceptions unless it's Margaret. I fly happily along in a single-engine puddlejumper with just Margaret at the controls. Back home, my staff may be worried sick about my breaking our rules on flying, but they don't know Margaret Ringenberg, the absolute best pilot in the world. I have long been fascinated by this remarkable woman, and know that many others will be delighted to read about her life.

Dan Coats
U.S. Senator from Indiana

Preface

I seldom attend aviation conferences or class reunions. I'd rather be flying. I went to the 1992 Women in Aviation Conference in Las Vegas, Nevada, because they wanted the younger women to meet some of us "old-timers," especially those of us who had been Women Airforce Service Pilots (WASP) in World War II. I scanned the list of seminar topics, but nothing captured my interest. Sitting through a session on "Airplane Mechanics" did not appeal to me. There was one on how to become a commercial airline pilot, but I had been flying for more than fifty years and wasn't anticipating a new career. I was wondering what to do with the rest of the day, when one topic, "The Learning Process," caught my eye. For some reason, that intrigued me. The speaker, Gary Eiff, was a professor at Purdue University and the husband of Mary Ann Eiff, a fellow pilot. Expecting him to be an interesting speaker, I joined his group.

He began by telling how he had taken his five-year-old granddaughter up in his airplane and let her fly it. It was his opinion that children decide early on what they are going to do in life. They may not be conscious of it, but something to which they have been exposed will influence their decisions later in life. I couldn't get that concept out of my mind after the conference ended. What had happened in my childhood to influence my decisions? What circumstances had led me, an Indiana farm girl, into what has been a lifelong adventure in aviation? I had never given it much thought before. I flew because I loved it, simple as that.

After more than fifty years of flying I had a room full of trophies from air races, including the prestigious Air Race Classic. I had been a WASP during World War II, ferrying planes all over the continental United States, and I could name drop with the best, having flown scores of interesting people, including the man who became our forty-fourth Vice president, Dan Quayle. But why had I chosen a career in aviation when other young women of my generation were aspiring to become secretaries, nurses, or teachers? I began to cast about in my memories, searching for clues about who I am. This book is a result of that search.

Margaret J. Ringenberg

PART ONE

Learning To Fly

"A girl nowadays must believe completely in herself as an individual. She must realize at the outset that a woman must do the same job better than a man to get as much credit for it. She must be aware of the various discriminations, both legal and traditional, against women in the business world."
--Amelia Earhart, Women's Career Counselor,
Purdue University (1935-1936)

✈

Girls Can't Be Pilots.
Can They?

I was about eight or nine years old when I took my first airplane ride. It might make for an interesting story to say that from that moment on, I set my sights on being a pilot, but that isn't how it happened. My mother and dad, two older sisters and I had gone for a Sunday drive, something families did more often in those days when gas was only ten cents a gallon. We were down around Berne, Indiana, when we saw a plane land in a farmer's field. While we were watching, the pilot crossed the field and asked, "Do you want to go for a ride?"

"Yes, yes!" we girls cried. Mother said no.

"How much?" Dad asked. I guess the price was right because Dad agreed. Mother resisted.

We persisted, and when she realized we were determined to go in spite of her misgivings, Mother reluctantly agreed. I remember her saying, "If the whole family is going to be killed, I want to die too."

I scrambled into the plane, envious of my dad, who got to sit up front where the man was flying the airplane. Was I interested even then in what made the plane go? The pilot flew us around and landed without incident, which was exciting, but it didn't change my life. At least, I didn't think so at the time. I didn't suddenly decide I wanted to grow up to be a pilot. There were a few women pilots at that time, Amelia Earhart, Bobbi Trout, Florence "Pancho" Barnes, but that meant nothing to me. I was too busy being a child to give any thought to the future. That flight was a novel way to spend a Sunday afternoon, nothing more.

I was born on June 17, 1921, in Fort Wayne, Indiana, to Albert and Lottie Ray. My two sisters, Violet and Mary, were seven and nine years older. My dad worked for General Electric, and like most women of her generation, my mother was a homemaker. After I started school in Fort Wayne, my parents bought an eighty-acre farm near Hoagland, about ten miles south of Fort Wayne, where my dad became a "gentleman farmer." He kept his job at General Electric and neighbors farmed our land on shares, growing corn and wheat. My sisters, who were teenagers then, had other interests, but I thrived on that farm. My dad bought a horse and taught me how to drive a tractor. We kept cows and chickens and tried our hands at making hay, our efforts bringing smiles to our neighbors at times. I did my share of farm chores alongside a succession of college students who worked for us as hired hands. When I was about fourteen, I would ride my bike to Hoagland to pick beans, and later I worked in a cannery there for seventeen cents an hour, good money back then! I did know that working in the cannery was not going to be my life's work; I broke out in a rash every time I got near a tomato or pineapple.

A few years later I became an entrepreneur. One summer my friend, Marian Crabill, and I decided to have a hamburger stand at the Hoagland Fair. Right away, the local tavern owner started complaining that we would cut into his lunch crowd. So while we were setting up our booth, some of the other vendors suggested to us that instead of selling hamburgers, we might want to provide hot meals for the other vendors. It sounded like a good idea. Consequently, for the duration of the Fair, we cooked chicken, mashed potatoes and gravy, and vegetables at home and brought them to the Fair to sell to the workers. Marian earned enough to buy an accordion and I made enough to take a trip to California with my sister, Violet.

I don't remember giving any more thought to airplanes until I was in junior high school, and then it was just idle fascination with the occasional airplane that flew over the school. One of my teachers later told my mother how I would watch the plane out the window, how my eyes would follow it until it was out of sight. Then I would go back to my schoolwork.

I guess I must have been about sixteen when I took my second plane ride. A friend, Kathleen Witmer, and I were out driving and somehow or other we ended up at Smith Field in Fort

21

Wayne. While we were sitting there in the car, someone, probably a young pilot trying to impress the girls, offered to take us for a plane ride, so we accepted the offer. We made the mistake of talking about it when we got home, and did we get a scolding — not because we went up in the airplane, but because we did it on Sunday! I had been attending First Missionary Church in Fort Wayne almost since birth, and the youth group there provided many activities of which my parents approved. Apparently, flying around in the sky on Sunday afternoon with a young man wasn't one of them.

I wasn't hooked on flying after that either, but I did start to entertain the idea of becoming a flight attendant. We called it a stewardess in those days. It still had not dawned on me that I could be a pilot. In fact, when I drove to California with my sister Violet and some friends to go to the World's Fair, we had our handwriting analyzed just for fun. "You're going to do something," the analyst predicted, "that takes a lot of coordination and smooth movements." I was sure I was going to dance on the stage!

Later in 1940, the senior edition of the Hoagland High School newspaper foretold, " . . a colorful future for Margaret Jane too. In years to come, people will not say 'Sonja Henie' in connection with ice skating. They will say Margaret Jane Ray. Her ingenious ability will add another star to the banner of Hoagland High School." So much for high school prophecies. However, I was also quoted as saying my ambition was to get a man with money. That's one goal I did reach when I married a banker. I guess I hadn't specified that it was to be his own money. Other girls in my class aspired to be secretaries, teachers, nurses, beauty operators, models, or housewives. The expectations of girls in 1940 rarely exceeded the boundaries set by society. World War II was to change all that.

The song listed in the program for my high school Baccalaureate service was 'And Who Will Our Pilot Be?' I don't think anyone thought it would be me.
— Margaret Ringenberg

What If The Pilot Has A Heart Attack?

After graduation in 1940 I began to give serious thought to becoming an airline stewardess. My fascination with flying had grown. Being a stewardess seemed the only way I could pursue my interest. When I discovered that nurse's training was part of the required course of study, Dad helped me get a job at General Electric to earn the money for nursing school. After completing my studies, I hoped to get a job with an airline.

My job at GE, "test and inspection," paid well, but it didn't require a hundred percent of my attention and my mind would wander. One day I had an unsettling thought. *What if I'm working as a stewardess some day and the pilot gets sick?*

*What if he has a heart attack? I really should learn
how to fly the airplane just in case.* I explained my
plan to my dad one day on the way home from
work. " I want to learn to fly an airplane," I announced. My dad just kept driving. It was as if he
wouldn't even dignify my announcement with a
response. I was devastated. Still I couldn't stop
thinking about the pilot and the hypothetical heart
attack. It was two weeks before I got up the nerve
to ask again.

As soon as I brought up the subject, my dad
rattled off the name of a flight school, the cost,
and other details I hadn't considered. I realized
he had heard me the first time. He didn't once try
to talk me out of it. Since we worked at the same
place, Dad and I rode to work together, but I started
an hour earlier than he did. When I got out of
work, I had to wait for him anyway, so we arranged
that I would go to the airport after work for flying
lessons.

There were three flight schools at Smith
Field near Fort Wayne: Inter-City, Johnny Whicker
Flight Service and Pierce Flying Service. Dad suggested Pierce because he had known the original
owner, Lloyd Pierce, from General Electric. Mr.
Pierce had been killed in 1938 so it was his widow
who was at the desk the day I walked into the
building that housed Pierce Flying Service and
announced, "I want to learn to fly." If there was a
turning point in my life, that was it.

"What would you like to fly?" she asked.
Thinking that "airplane" was probably not the
answer she wanted, I hesitated.

"Something small," I said. I started taking
lessons for six dollars an hour in the fall of 1941. I

never did get around to nurse's training.

Fred Bunyan
(FORMER OFFICE MANAGER
PIERCE FLYING SERVICE)

I didn't have an instructor's rating when Margaret first came out to Smith Field. Whitey Fry and his brothers ran the service; I was the office manager. Whitey had an annoying habit of "stealing the thunder" from the other guys. I saw him do it many times. He would watch the other instructors' students, and when he saw one that looked about ready to solo, Whitey would pull a fast one and take the student up for a check ride and solo him before the regular instructor got a chance. I never thought to warn Margaret about him.

Surprisingly, no one questioned my decision to learn to fly, even though women were a bit of a novelty at the air field back then. Three brothers, Whitey, Kenny and Danny Fry, had purchased and now owned the flying service. Danny was my first instructor. I soon found out that learning to fly was different from learning to drive. Flying was done by "feel." I would sit in the back seat with my hand on the stick. Danny, in the front seat, would move his stick, which would move mine. After awhile he would release his and let me control the airplane, but he could take it back at any time.

After about a dozen thirty-minute lessons, I was feeling fairly confident. Danny mentioned to Whitey that he thought I would be ready to solo before long. Then one day when I went for my lesson, it was Whitey, not Danny, who climbed into the plane with me. "Danny isn't going to be here today," he said. "I'm going to be your instructor." I never thought to question it; after all, he was one of the owners. The plane was a J-3 Cub, one of the little yellow planes so often seen at small airports. We took it up and went around the field a couple of times, and when we landed, Whitey got out. "Take it around," he ordered.

"Alone?" I protested. "No, I can't!"

He insisted.

"No," I repeated. "I'm not ready!"

I don't want to repeat the words he used then, but he scared me so badly, I shut the door, took off and soloed. I was thrilled and nervous, and more than a little annoyed, but I did it. I got on the ground safely and picked up Whitey. "I'm not supposed to solo yet," I explained to him. "I don't have eight hours." Then he cussed me out for not having told him I didn't have the required number of hours. "You never asked," I said. I often wonder what words Danny used when he got back from the phony errand Whitey had sent him on that day.

Soloing had been my immediate goal. I hadn't thought much beyond that. Everything about flying excited me and I was spending nearly all my spare time at the airport. I was still working at General Electric, but if I wanted something to do, I went to the airport just to watch the planes and listen to the "hangar talk." The pilots had a lingo all their own and I wanted to be a part of that. My course was set; I just didn't know it yet.

✈

I Just Want To Fly

There wasn't any possibility by then that I would quit flying. I still wasn't thinking of it as a career, but I knew I wanted to fly every chance I got. As luck would have it, in the summer of 1942 I had the opportunity to become part owner of a J-3 Cub trainer. After all these years I still remember the numbers on that plane — 35735. There were three of us, Johnny Haines, Harley Shaefer, and I, sharing the plane as well as the cost of parking, insurance, and maintenance. We had a schedule for when each member could fly it, which was the best way to get flying time at the least possible cost.

As I began to accumulate flying hours, it just seemed the natural thing to go ahead and get my private license, which would entitle me to carry passengers, although not for hire. We went to Indiana Technical College in Fort Wayne for ground school. There weren't many girls there and the instructor clearly didn't appreciate my presence, but Freddie Bunyan was there and he always came to my defense. In fact, I had a lot of friends there who "took me under their wings," so to speak. At that time, Civilian Pilot Training was paying for the training of some civilian pilots, but I paid for my own.

I was sitting in the coffee shop at Smith Field on December 7, 1941, when the news of Pearl Harbor reached us. We had no way of knowing then how that "date that will live in infamy" would change our lives. The immediate effect was that all civilian flying was suspended. I had to apply to the Civil Aeronautics Authority (CAA) to get my student pilot certificate reinstated. Clarence McNabb, an attorney and friend of my parents, wrote a letter of reference for me assuring the government that I was not a threat to national security. Flying became quite complicated for awhile. Gas and spare parts were hard to come by. American airports were placed under armed guard to prevent saboteurs from stealing planes and bombing war plants. Civilian pilots often had to prove their citizenship and loyalty before planes could be cleared for takeoff. This sometimes meant convincing the weather bureau that the pilot was not Japanese. Then the security guard would have to be convinced that the pilot was only out for practice and that his or her license had been reinstated by the CAA. The guard would check it out if he hadn't lost the pilot's file. By the time he cut through all the red tape, it was sometimes too late in the day to fly.

Late in 1941, a plan was approved to organize civilian pilots. In Europe all civilian aviation activity had stopped when the war had begun. American fliers didn't want that to happen in the United States so they set out to prove that civilian aviation had a role to play in the country's defense. The Civil Air Patrol (CAP) was born. Because a decrease in civilian flying would mean the closing of many local airports, the Army Air Force would lose fields that could be used by military pilots in an emergency. To forestall such eventualities the military called on the Civil Air Patrol to keep those airports open. This could mean simply keeping the grass cut, potholes filled and hangars repaired, or it could mean just paying for enough instruction to warrant keeping the field open.

There was to be a CAP wing in each state. Each wing had squadrons of fifty to two hundred which were divided into flights of ten to sixty members each. While any citizen over the age of eighteen and of good character could enlist, the first call was for men and women who could fly or who had some special skill like radio operators or mechanics. I was one of the first in the Fort Wayne area to sign up. We went to the armory for training, which included military drills. I could not foresee, of course, that eventually the discipline would help me become a section leader during WASP training. Since it was a new concept, our leaders seemed to be learning right along with the rest of us.

The Civil Air Patrol was supposed to be serious business. After all, there had been reports of German submarine activity in coastal areas. In Fort Wayne, however, the threat of foreign saboteurs seemed a little less imminent. There was more than a little satire on the subject of sabotage in the March 1942 issue of CAP Flights. "Saboteurs in wood-lot northwest of the airport," one reporter wrote. "Suspicious looking huts near farmhouse — bomb shelters or pig houses. No anti-aircraft fire over Columbia City. No submarine activity in the Fort Wayne rivers." All kidding aside, I know now that if Smith Field had not been designated by the CAA, I probably would not have had the means to complete my private license later in 1942. Timing, I learned, was everything,

✈

Things I Never Told My Mother

I became ill one day at work in February 1943. Thinking I was coming down with the flu, I went to the company doctor. "It isn't the flu," he said as he pressed my side. "You have appendicitis." Just about that time, a fellow came in with his thumb cut off. Everybody turned their attention to him, and since I had not given my name when I reported to the doctor, I just walked out and went back to work. That doctor didn't know what he was talking about, I grumped. I just had the flu. A little later I mentioned the doctor's comment to some of the older ladies. "Appendicitis can be serious," they told me. "You had better do something about it." Since I wasn't feeling any better when I got home, I told my folks. They sent me to the family doctor in New Haven, who sent me straight to the hospital, where I remained for seven days following surgery. Obviously it was a slow news week in Fort Wayne because the News Sentinel reported, "Margaret Ray is. . . convalescing satisfactorily at Lutheran Hospital, where she underwent an appendectomy." During that time, of course, I didn't get to fly or go to the airport. That was probably the worst part for me.

When I had been home from the hospital only a few days, I talked my folks into letting me drive out to the airport. " Just to visit," I said. I couldn't stay away any longer. When I got to the airport, though, I wanted to go flying. Freddie Bunyan was there and if I wanted to go flying, he was going to do everything he could to help me. I wasn't in pain, but I was still a little tender. Crawling over the frame into the little J-3 Cub was going to be uncomfortable, I told Freddie. He went out to the hangar and when he came back he said, "I got the Stinson." The Stinson, a single-engine tail dragger, was powered by either 90 or 100 horsepower, but I had only a 0-80-horsepower rating and so did Freddie. He worked at the airport as a lineman and did some instructing, so he could take the Stinson up alone, but it was not legal for him to carry passengers. He had simply gone and checked out the plane and, assuming he was going alone, no one asked any questions.

We had to go around behind the hangar to get the airplane, and there was Harley Shaefer hanging around as usual. " I want to go too," he said. "That airplane has three seats." We were afraid he'd tell if we didn't take him, so Freddie got into the left seat; I was in the right and Harley climbed into the jump seat in back. We taxied it out and got up in the air and then, naturally, I wanted to fly it. Freddie knew me well. He knew I couldn't go up in an airplane and not want to fly it, so, although it was against regulations, he had put in a second yoke for me to fly from the right seat.

I decided to do some stalls. A stall occurs when the pilot pulls back on the wheel and brings the nose up until the air speed dissipates and the airplane won't fly anymore. It is not a stalling of the engine, but of the plane itself. If the pilot keeps holding back on the wheel, the weight of the airplane will bring the nose down and the airplane will pick up a little speed. Then the nose will go back up and the airplane will stall again. This pattern will continue with the plane losing altitude each time until the pilot pushes forward on the wheel. The purpose is to understand the airplane and how to land it since every landing is actually a stall very close to the ground. So I did a couple of stalls, but when I tried to go forward on the wheel again to pick up speed, the wheel wouldn't move. The nose dropped down. We managed to use the throttle to bring the nose up, but when we'd throttle back, the nose would come down again. We tried to direct it back to the field, and we were all plenty worried.

First of all, Freddie had gone out back of the hangar to get the airplane. None of us would say it, but I was thinking that maybe it had been out there because there was something wrong with it. We were afraid if we forced it and there was a bolt out of the elevator or something, we could have more serious trouble than we already had. Secondly, none of us was legal on the plane. Harley and I started to accuse Freddie of not line-checking it well enough. "I went out and put the second yoke in it," he said. "I didn't see anything wrong with it."

We were just northwest of Fort Wayne by old Highway 30 when Freddie made a decision: "I'm going to try to land it using the throttle. When I tell you, cut off the gas." I did as he said, and we landed safely, but what a predicament! There I was, fresh out of the hospital. We were sitting in the middle of a farmer's field, and none of us was legal on the plane. Nobody wanted to get into trouble, especially Freddie, because he had signed the airplane out. We had to do some quick plotting. Freddie would go to a farmhouse west of the field, and Harley and I would head south across the field to another house. When we came to a fence, I recalled that we were in this mess because I hadn't felt like climbing into the J-3. Under the circumstances, however, I thought I should climb the fence. We went up to a house and told the woman who came to the door that somebody would be picking us up shortly. Could we sit on her porch for a little while?

We sat on her porch for a long while! Presently we watched as a car crossed the field. People got out and walked around the plane. After awhile, someone got in and took off. The rest of the people got in the car and drove away. We couldn't see who was flying the plane, what had happened or anything. Hours went by and Freddie did not return. Neither of us had money for a cab so we decided to start walking. I thought about the J-3 again and how I was now going to walk three miles because I hadn't wanted to climb into the little plane.

Finally, about four or five hours after he had left us, Freddie came down the road in a car and picked us up. "Where have you been?" we demanded. He explained that he had reported the forced landing to the CAA as required and they had come with a mechanic to check it out. The mechanic found that the pin that held the second yoke was in backwards. He fixed it and flew the plane back to the airport. Being a little suspicious, I suppose, the inspectors insisted on taking Freddie to lunch at a place called the Circle Bar. They probably thought they could loosen him up and he would "spill the beans."

"I had to eat," Freddie explained. "I couldn't very well tell them you were out here, and I didn't know whose house it was, so I couldn't call you." The inspectors had to know when they saw the other yoke in the plane that Freddie had not been alone. I guess they got tired of waiting for him to admit it, and let him go. My parents may have wondered why I was gone so long, but then when I went to the airport, it wasn't unusual for me not to come back right away. I don't remember if either of them ever asked. I know I never told.

✈

Impossible Dream

IF INTERESTED IN WOMEN FLYING TRAINING FOR
FERRY COMMAND CONTACT ME PALMER HOUSE
CHICAGO TUESDAY THRU THURSDAY FEBRUARY
16TH 17TH 18TH FOR INTERVIEW AGE LIMITS 21 TO
34 INCLUSIVE AMOUNT OF TRAINING INCREASED
PRIVATE LICENSE ADMITS TO EARLY CLASS PLEASE
TELL OTHER WOMEN PILOTS.
    ETHEL SHEEHY CHIEF RECRUITING OFFICER

E arly in February 1943 our neighbor girl came running up to the house calling, "There's a telegram for Margaret Jane Ray and she's to call Western Union." We didn't have a telephone so the telegram had been delivered to the neighbor whose phone number I had put on my application for a private license. I couldn't imagine what it was all about. I didn't even know anyone who had received a telegram before. Telegrams were the means of notifying families of a loved one missing in action so I assumed it must be bad news of some sort. I should have been ecstatic when I found out what it was, but it was all so unreal I wasn't sure how to react.

Three other women in the area received the

same telegram. One was Gene Garvin, whom I had met when she came out to Pierce for flying lessons. Like me, once she had a taste she was hooked. She had once worked at the TWA office at the airport just so she could be near the airplanes. When the telegram came, she was working as Senior Control Operator, directing traffic at Smith Field. Mary McKinley from Fort Wayne Aero Club was on her way to getting a commercial license and instructor's rating when she received her telegram. The third was Loretta Foellinger, whose family owned Fort Wayne Newspapers. I was still recovering from my appendectomy and asked the other girls to wait for me. We took the train up to Chicago on the last possible day. It was the first of many train rides I would take in the next few years.

In the interview, Mrs. Ethel Sheehy explained what the Women's Flying Training Detachment (WFTD) was all about and then questioned me about my flying experience and background. All of us passed the interview and Mrs. Sheehy instructed us on how to apply. We could not conceal our excitement on the way home. It seemed like a dream. Was it possible that such a dream could come true? A few days later I received a letter from Jacqueline Cochran, Director of Women's Flying Training, explaining that "upon clearance of your Civil Service appointment and approval of your medical examination, you will be officially notified when and where to report for duty."

When we reported to Baer Field in early March for our flight physicals, Mary didn't pass. I think she was more interested in instructing than ferry work, but still she must have been disappointed. Then Loretta dropped out under pressure from her family. I suppose they thought it was too dangerous for a young woman. Ironically, Loretta was killed some years later in a crash of a private plane. My mother was silent on the subject of the WFTD. I think she knew that if I had my mind made up, I would do it. After all, I was twenty-one years old, even if I was the baby of the family. "I was never able to serve," my dad told me. "It looks like you will be the one in the family to do it." I never thought about what I would have done if my parents had been against my decision. I suppose they thought there were worse things I could do. Even so, after I left, my parents got a lot of criticism from other people.

"She must have been unhappy at home," someone told my mother, "or she wouldn't have gone into the Service." Others questioned my character as well. Nice girls didn't go into the Service. In fact, nice girls didn't leave home at all unless it was to marry.

It was down to Gene and me. The physical was the same one required of all Army Air Force cadets, males who were prospective fighter pilots. I had explained to the interviewer in Chicago that it had been only a couple of weeks since my surgery. Mrs. Sheehy had assured me that the Army allowed six weeks for recovery time and that if accepted, I could just wait until the April class to report. I didn't volunteer any information to the doctor, however, and it was late into the exam before he noticed the incision. By that time, I had stepped on and off a chair several times and had performed every test he required. He signed the medical for the March class. Soon thereafter the newspaper carried the good news: I was the first "girl" from the Fort Wayne area to be accepted into the Army Air Force Flying Training Detachment (AAFTD). Gene, who was from Payne, Ohio, made it too. We awaited orders to report to Sweetwater, Texas.

The original Women's Auxiliary Ferrying Squadron, under the leadership of Nancy Love, had begun in September 1942. Only the most experienced pilots were admitted. Most of them had at least a thousand hours of flying experience. Many could have qualified as commercial airline pilots if the airlines hired women. But I was to be known as one of "Jackie's girls." It was Jackie Cochran, at the urging of General H.H "Hap" Arnold, who had provided the opportunity for those of us with less experience. She began interviewing pilots for the WFTD. At first she anticipated being able to accept only those with commercial licenses or three hundred hours, but before long the demand for women ferry pilots had become so great that the requirements were reduced to a private license. I had a private license, thanks to the fellows at Smith Field. When the men began leaving for the armed services, it created a shortage of instructors. I think the plan was to hurry me along so that I could get my instructor's rating and help keep the flying service going through the war. Fortunately, whenever someone at Smith Field needed a plane moved, they would let me fly it to give me more air time. Little did any of us know that I would leave for service before many of them.

The next weeks passed in a flurry of activity. There was no time for any fanfare, no parties,

41

no grand send-off. In fact, we had been instructed not to publicize what we were about to do as we didn't want the enemy to know that the United States was so desperate that it was training women! The day I left is rather a blur to me now. It may be that my dad drove me to the train station or, wanting to avoid an emotional farewell, I may have driven myself and left the car at the station to be picked up later. Whichever, afterwards I learned that my dog had followed the car that day and had never gone home.

I think my older sister, Violet, was affected a great deal by my leaving. Mary had gotten married in 1940 so when I left, Violet was the only one of us still at home. Without the knowledge of the family, she went to the airport and got Freddie Bunyan to give her flying lessons. She admitted later that she never intended to become a pilot or even earn a private license; she just wanted to solo. It seemed that everyone else was doing something exciting and she didn't want to be left out. Eventually she joined the Red Cross because of her desire to contribute to the war effort.

ANOTHER VOICE:

Mary Thompson
(SISTER)

It's difficult for me to think of Margaret Jane
as a celebrity. She's my sister. Growing up she
was just one of the family. While my sister Vi and
I enjoyed doing things in the house, Margaret Jane
never did. She preferred working in the barn and
driving the tractor or car, so when she decided to
take flying lessons, it was nothing out of the ordinary to us. We just accepted the fact that we were
all different. Vi was a gardener while my interests were more in the area of home decorating;
Margaret Jane liked to fly. She was always braver
than I was. I didn't even like to drive the car unless I had to. When Vi and Margaret Jane drove to
the World's Fair in California with friends years
ago, my dad just couldn't understand why I didn't
want to go with them. He even offered to pay my
way, but I said, "No, if I wanted to go I'd pay my
own way." I was saving my money to get married!

While some people may have thought it odd
for a woman to join the Service at that time, I did
not. Of course, I was lonesome for her when she
left; it was strange to go out to the house and not
have her there. I didn't, however, worry about her.
After all, she was only doing what she had always
done. She made a point of telling us that if anything happened to her while she was flying, we
should remember that she was happy. Consequently I have never been nervous about her flying. I'm not afraid to fly *with* her either. Today when
someone asks me if I'm proud of her, I reply that I

am, but I was just as proud of Vi for the things that she did. Other people may focus on Margaret Jane's accomplishments, but to me she is just my sister, and I'm glad that she is able to do what makes her happy.

PART TWO

Flying For My Country

"Women may not have any big role in post-war commercial aviation, but there's a job for us to do today, and we must exert every energy to do it well." Jackie Cochran

✈

The WASP

W e were class 43W-5, meaning the fifth class of 1943. We were also the first class who would start and complete our training at Sweetwater, Texas. All the classes before us had begun their training in Houston. Before our arrival, the base had been used to train male British cadets, and there was still one class of U.S. cadets at Sweetwater when we arrived. To maintain a strict segregation of the sexes quartered there, we had to fly from opposite ends of the field. We weren't even supposed to look at the boys, but our living quarters were next door to theirs, so orders or no orders, we looked. When they left a few weeks later, Avenger Field became the only all-female air base in United States history.

The trainee barracks were divided into two rooms called bays, a name given them by the British cadets. There was a bathroom between the rooms, which housed six women each. That meant twelve young women sharing one bathroom! Our beds were regulation Army cots, sharing space with a built-in study desk, straight chairs, and pine board lockers. Not exactly the Ritz, but I soon found out I wouldn't be spending enough time in the room to care.

If I was homesick, I didn't have time to dwell on it. Reveille sounded at six o'clock the next morning and I was in the army. Suddenly I felt very inadequate among others who had more education and experience than I had. Only a few days before, we had been secretaries, factory workers, nurses, teachers and, in more than a few cases, farm girls; but if people thought the military went easier on us because we were women, they were mistaken. The training was intense. It had to be. In six months we were going to be asked to complete the training it took male cadets nine months to finish. In all fairness to the men, however, our shortened time was due to the fact that all of us had been pilots before joining.

Years later when the women began to push for military recognition of the Women Airforce Service Pilots (WASP), I was disturbed by an article in a newspaper quoting a spokesman from the Veteran's Administration. "The WASP were not subject to military discipline or orders, nor were they limited to military pay," he said. "As a result they were never considered components of the armed forces." This simply was not true. In every way our training was identical to that of the male cadets except for gunnery training. Some WASPs did get the dubious honor of towing targets for the men to shoot at, however. We also skipped over certain fundamentals because we already knew how to fly.

I was not originally a WASP. It was not until August 1943 that the WFTD and the Women's Auxiliary Flying Service (WAFS) merged to become the WASP, but we were trainees of the Army Air Force and as such we were expected to stand roll call and barracks inspection. We took the same oath as the male cadets. We marched to breakfast, to the flight line, to ground school and physical training. Upon arrival in Sweetwater, we were asked, "Who has marched before?" Having marched at the armory in Fort Wayne while in the Civil Air Patrol, I raised my hand. Consequently, I became the flight leader, calling cadence everywhere we marched. I think I would have marched in my sleep if I had had the energy, but a day that began as early as 6 a.m. could end as late as 10 p.m. Incidentally, I never raised my hand after that! We ate Army chow, lived in barracks, could not leave the base without a pass, and received demerits for infractions such as dust under the bed, wrinkles in the bedding, or improper dress. Jackie insisted on the military discipline because she didn't want anyone to say that the women couldn't pull their own weight. We were expected to conform to a rigid code of conduct. Some could take it; some couldn't. We were volunteers, however, so there was nothing to keep us from leaving if we decided we'd had enough. Even so, the rate of attrition for women trainees was about thirty-five percent, no higher than that of the men.

There was no official uniform when I joined, but earlier classes had adopted khaki trousers, white shirts, and khaki overseas caps as the unofficial uniform of the WFTD. I should say that those were our dress uniforms. Our flight suits, provided by the Army, were another story. They were leftover men's coveralls, the smallest of which was size 40. We called them zoot suits and they were a daily reminder that we were there to do a job, not look glamorous. Incidentally, we all paid about one hundred dollars out of our own pockets to outfit ourselves. We were issued caps, goggles, coveralls, jackets and parachutes. Everything else we paid for ourselves out of one hundred fifty dollars a month pay, including our transportation to Sweetwater and $1.65 a day for room and board. If this is what our detractor meant by "not subject to military pay," then he was partially correct.

The first day we were divided into flights. When our flight training began in earnest the next day, half us were flying or waiting to fly, while the others went to ground school. The rest of the day was spent in physical training, marching on the drill field, or in the Link trainer, which was basically a crude flight simulator mounted on a base which permitted the trainer to tilt and turn. For five hours a day we studied math, physics, meteorology, navigation, aerodynamics, electronics and instruments, military and civilian air regulations, engine operations and maintenance. When we weren't in class or in the air, we were studying — on the flight line, between classes, and under the covers with a flashlight after bed check. Sometimes there were two or three exams a week, but to our credit no woman ever "washed out" for failing ground school. After the completion of ground school, I had what amounted to a college degree in aeronautics. Even though I never went to college, I have always felt that my WASP training gave me everything a college education could have, and more.

Avenger Field was an Army Air Force (AAF) base commanded by an Army major and administered by Army staff. Our instructors, however, were civilians, employees of the War Training Service. Some of them didn't like the idea of training females, but their jobs were keeping them out of combat, so it doesn't seem that the sex of their students should have mattered to them. I like to think that we were at least prettier than some of their former students.

Before Sweetwater, the only plane I had flown, with the exception of the ill-fated Stinson, was the little yellow J-3 Cub, which has a seat in the front and one in the back and a stick control. I had only my 0-80-horsepower rating. We began our training in the PT-19A, a 175-horsepower open-cockpit trainer with a cruising speed of 90 miles per hour. Seat belts were mandatory since, when the plane turned over in the air, a girl could, and sometimes did, fall out! Although it was one of the smaller trainers, the PT-19 seemed huge to me. The cockpit procedures, a page long, were intimidating and confusing until I realized that all airplanes, regardless of size, basically flew the same. In about two weeks, we began soloing the PT-19, after which we could take it up by ourselves.

We then moved on to the BT-13 with a 450-horsepower Wright engine. And I had thought the PT 19 was huge! It was big and cumbersome and had a bad reputation. Named the "Valiant" by the manufacturer, it was sometimes referred to as the "Vultee Vibrator" by the students, who complained that it rattled and shook and was unreliable in a spin. The cruising speed was 130 miles per hour and it landed at 90! Unlike the PT 19, it had an enclosed canopy top, a radio, and about three pages of cockpit procedures to learn, but once again I survived the check.

The AT-6 Texan , a single-engine advanced trainer, was the next hurdle in our training. This was the first trainer we had flown with retractable landing gear. It had 650-horsepower and cruised at 145 miles per hour, quite an exciting change from the J-3 Cub. The long solo cross-country flights in the AT 6 gave me my first glimpse of my future as a ferry pilot, and I loved it! Finally we flew the AT-17 (UC-78), a twin engine Cessna Bobcat, nicknamed the "Bamboo Bomber" because of its plywood and canvas construction. We spent hours taking off, flying a fixed course, and then landing again and again until we could do it the Army way.

"If Hitler could see what he is up against now, the war might be shortened considerably."--Major Gen. Gerald C. Brant at WFTD graduation (Flying, July 1943)

(Editor's note: The following cockpit procedures for the PT 19-A and BT-15 are taken from the actual instructions given to WFTD trainees. Punctuation, spelling, and emphasis are original.)

PT 19-A

1. Check and fill out Form 1.
2. As you pick up each safety belt, call out the amount of gas
3. in each tank.
4. Safety belt fastened
5. Gosports connected
6. Seat Adjusted
    Then move your attention to the controls
1. Rudder adjusted
2. Controls unlocked and free
3. Parking brakes set
    Then move your attention to the left side of the ship
    Start with
1. Flaps up and locked
2. Wobble pump handle down (pump the wobble pump a few times)
3. Trim tab, set zero
4. Mixture rich
5. Gas on left or right tank (call amount of gas in that tank)
6. Set throttle (pump throttle two or three times)
7. Call out "ready" to starter, starter will call "contact"
    You shall call "contact left mag."
8. When engine starts you shall control engine RPM then
    switch to both mags

LEAVING PARKING LINE

1. Release parking brakes, look out in front, add throttle, taxi away.
2. As you leave line check Tee and tower, then proceed to take off position
3. Line up 45 deg. to take off position

RUN A BRIEF COCKPIT CHECK
1. Including flaps up, trim tab set, mixture rich, gas and the tank selected for take off
2. Carburetor heat cold. altimeter set zero, fuel pressure, oil pressure, temperature checked.
3. Run engine to 1400 RPM
4. Check mags from both to left back to both then to right then back to both

TAKE OFF
1. Look around good then check tower and Tee
2. Line up and take off

BT 15
COCKPIT PROCEDURE
(Note: Although we flew B-13's, the cockpit procedure for the 15 is similar.)
CHECK FOR STARTING
1. Check form I
2. As you pick up each safety belt call out gas supply in each tank.
3. Fasten safety belt
4. Adjust seat
5. Plug in earphones
6. Check radio switches off
THEN MOVE ATTENTION TO CONTROLS SIDE OF COCKPIT
1. Adjust rudders

2. Controls unlocked and free
3. Set parking brakes

THEN MOVE ATTENTION TO LEFT SIDE OF COCKPIT
1. Flaps up
2. Rudder 0 deg or 3 deg. R.
3. Trim tab) deg
4. Gas on RESERVE
5. Throttle Cracked 1/2 in.
6. Mixture full rich
7. Prop high pitch - full back
8. Carburetor full cold
9. Oil shutter as desired
10. Check instruments

STARTING

1. Wobble pump S-L-O-W-L-Y to 3 or 4 lbs.
2. Prime 2 or 3 times when hot: 4 to 5 when cold
3. Switch on BOTH
4. Energize to peak only
5. Before engaging "clear" must be called out loudly out both sides
6. Engage
7. When oil pressure is up to 50 lbs., prop full forward
8. Check fuel pressure and oil pressure; if no oil after ten seconds, shut engine off
9. Radio on
10. Gen. switch on

TAKE OFF

1. Check mags 1500 R.P.M.
2. Check trims and gas on reserve — 20 deg flaps

3. Check altimeters
4. Throttle full open smoothly for take off

CLIMB
1. Climb with 20 deg flaps to desired altitude
2. Climb in low pitch (take off position) 2100 R.P.M.
3. Gas on fuller tank

CRUISING
1. Crank flaps up
2. Propeller HIGH PITCH
3. Cruise 1850 R.P.M.
4. Mixture control as desired

CLIMB
1. Climb with 20 deg flaps to desired altitude
2. Climb in low pitch (takeoff position) 2100 R.P.M.

CRUISING
1. Crank flaps up
2. Propeller HIGH PITCH
3. Cruise 1850 R.P.M.
4. Mixture control as desired

LANDING
1. Mixture full rich
2. Gas on RESERVE
3. Carburetor full cold
4. Propeller full low pitch
5. Place flaps at 20 deg
6. Flaps as needed
7. After landing FLAPS UP

STOPPING
1. Set parking brakes
2. Throttle 1500 R.P.M.
3. Propeller high pitch

4. Mixture full lean
5. Switch off -- Gen. switch off
6. Lock controls -- 20 deg flaps
7. Fill out Form I

* ALL ALTIMETERS WILL BE SET FOR SEA LEVEL
SETTING BEFORE TAKING OFF ON ALL BASIC
OPERATIONS (2376 FT. SWEETWATER)

✈

Silver Wings, Silver Screen

Not many people know I was in the movies. One, titled "Unusual Occupations," was made at Avenger Field, but to this day I haven't seen it. My real claim to fame on the silver screen came while I was stationed at Sweetwater. I'd like to say it was my great beauty that caused me to be chosen for the role, but in all likelihood it was my home address that destined me for stardom.

I was a member of the First Missionary Church in Fort Wayne at the time. People from the congregation wanted to write to the service people, and I suppose they asked my parents for my address and information about what I was doing. We were not supposed to release that information lest it fall into the hands of the enemy. However, I went up to the front office to see the Public Relations Officer to ask if my name and address could be published in the church bulletin at home. "Ah, you're from Indiana," he said when he saw the address. "I'm from Indianapolis." He told me that he had worked for the *Indianapolis Star* before the war. The government must have decided by then that information about the WFTD was not a threat to national security, and I was given permission to release my name and address.

Some time later, a movie company came to the base, filming for a movie called "Silver Wings." When the directors went to the Public Relations office to get someone to be in the movie, the good captain gave them my name. I guess he thought if someone was going to be in the movie, it might as well be a fellow Hoosier. I sat in an airplane, and they jacked up the tail and tied the plane down. The propeller was turning and my hair was blowing. It was supposed to look as though I was really flying. There were also a few shots on the flight line. It was all pretty silly and I didn't give it much thought when it was over.

Then one day I was assigned to pick up an L-4 "Grasshopper" at Piper in Lockhaven, Pennsylvania and take it to Kansas. The L-4, which was the Army designation for a Piper Cub, was slow with a cruising speed of about 75 miles per hour and not very glamorous, but I didn't care. I was an eager beaver; I would fly anything with wings. There were other girls in my flight and also a flight of fellows. We did not fly with the men, but following the flight, we all ended up in the same little town. We decided to go to a movie and what was showing but "Silver Wings." When it came on, my friends all screamed, "Look, Maggie! That's you!" I was so embarrassed; I ducked my head and refused to look. I regret now that I never got to see it. But for all I know, maybe there is a copy of that movie somewhere in the film archives. After all, it was history.

✈

A Near Washout

There were check rides at each phase of training. First, we would get a check ride from the civilian instructor, but to finish training we had to take an official Army test flight with a military check pilot. If the check ride was unsatisfactory, we received a pink slip with a big "U" on it. After a few more days of practice, we would get a second check ride, the elimination or E-ride. If we failed that, we washed out and were eliminated from the training program.

When I went into the WFTD and was instructed not to tell people why I was going into the service, I assumed it was because the government didn't want anyone to know the U.S. was desperate enough to hire women. Later, though, I suspected that it might be because they didn't want a lot of publicity due to the number of girls who were destined to "wash out." Indeed, our instructors told us going in that probably only one in three would make it. Nevertheless, eighty-five of the one hundred twenty-seven in Class 43 W-5 graduated, so I guess we did a little better than expected.

Every morning, as section leader I would call out names to make sure everyone was there, and then we would march to breakfast. Some mornings a girl just wouldn't be there anymore, and that would be the first we knew about it. When someone washed out, she would go back to the bay while the rest of us were over on the flight line, empty out her locker, close up her bed and leave. Sometimes she didn't see anyone or even say goodbye. There wasn't any rule about it, but most girls were so disappointed they didn't want to face anyone. We were lucky that everyone in our bay graduated, but that wasn't true of every bay. Sometimes, even now, I meet women who are hesitant to admit they had WASP training if they didn't graduate. I always felt bad when someone washed out, but for the most part I didn't have time to dwell on it.

Every day we would go over to the flight line and the assignments would be on the board with the name of our instructor. We didn't dare leave the line in case one of our names was called, so we would take our books and study or stretch out on a bench to catch a few minutes of sleep. I would meet someone and we would strike up a conversation, but in six months of concentrated training there wasn't much time to develop a close friendship with anyone other than my baymates. There was a lot of stress involved, never knowing if and when we might be eliminated. This little tune from my WASP days, author unknown, says it all:

> Check flight instructor was after me today.
> Too late for me to get on my knees and pray.
> Oh, how he spun me, now you must shun me,
> Check flight instructor was after me today.
>
> Clothes packed, I'm leaving, my flying days are done.
> Home to raise babies, the Army says it's fun.
> Making tiny garments, luck to you, you varmints,
> Check flight instructor has washed me out today.
> OOOoooh!

I remember one close call I had. I was still recovering from my appendectomy when I started training. As mentioned, in the PT-19, an open-cockpit primary trainer, it was necessary to pull the seat belt tight to keep from falling out of the plane when flying upside down. The belt was wide and each time I tightened it, it put pressure on my incision. I had a pillow I used to put behind me so that I could reach better, which was permissible, but I had placed the pillow in front of me and pulled the belt over it so it wouldn't hurt so much. On this occasion, the instructor, Jimmy Hill, who was in the back seat, jumped out and came up to the front. Right away he wanted to know why I had the pillow there. "I just had my appendix out in February," I explained. "It's a little sensitive when I put strain on the belt."

He was understanding and said, "We don't have to do that maneuver anymore." I can't remember now what the maneuver in question was, but I guess we didn't do it anymore and I was able to put the pillow back behind me. Just something like that could have caused me to be put up for an E-ride, but it was after I checked out on the primary and moved on to the basic trainer that I had my first real close call, and it was all because of the kindness of Jimmy Hill.

As luck would have it, the first thing my new instructor did was take me through that very maneuver. I was weak on it, of course, since Jimmy hadn't required me to do it. Then when we came back to the field to do some landings, my landings weren't so good either. The basic trainer, BT-13, was a much bigger airplane and the way it felt when I moved the controls just wasn't right. Anyway, the instructor put me up for a check ride. When the military check pilot who was to give me the E-ride got in the plane, I was really scared. Everything was riding on that test. If we got up there and the instructor found me lacking, my training days were over. " Okay," he said. "We'll go up and do a two-turn spin to the left, then a two-turn spin to the right. Then we'll do a chandelle and a lazy eight." He added a few more directions and I did everything he told me. When I headed back to the field, I knew my performance was within acceptable limits until I came in to land and BOUNCED! I picked up my mike and said, "The airplane didn't feel the way it did before."

"Do you think you could do it better if you tried again?" he asked. I said that I could and we took off and went around again. The next landing was acceptable, but I wasn't satisfied.

"I can do better than that," I told him. So up we went again and that time my landing was the way I wanted it.

"Okay, let's go in," he said. After I had parked the plane, he got out and walked into the ready room without saying a word to me. Jimmy Hill was there. "She says the airplane doesn't fly like it did before," the check pilot told Jim, ignoring me. "She proved she can land it, but I don't like her attitude. She's too cocky."

"No," said Jim, "I know her. She's not cocky. If she says there's something wrong, there is." They went back to check on who my instructor had been in Basic. They discovered that there had been complaints from other students about the "feel" of the plane. Jim decided it wasn't the plane that was the problem; it was the instructor. More than likely during training the instructor had ridden the controls. Then when I took my check ride, the military instructor had just let go of the controls and let me do it. It didn't feel the same. As soon as I had gotten the feel of it, I landed it correctly. Obviously the first instructor had skipped over one of the guidelines for flight instructors:

AIR CORRECTION.— Control riding. Dangers.—The instructor must not "ride" the controls when presumably the student is responsible for the performance of the airplane.

I wasn't eliminated, but right there when we came back from the check ride, the instructor could have sent me back to pack up my gear. The other girls would never have known what happened.

The same could be said for accidents, and there were a few during training. Indeed, eleven girls, not all from my class, died during training.

65

Just before graduation, we were all trying to get in some extra flying time in the AT-17's before we had to take our check rides. During a routine practice session, one of the planes went down, killing two trainees and the instructor. The Army did a good job of downplaying the incident. I didn't know the people involved personally. Although I surely realized there was danger involved in what I was doing, I didn't think about dying. Other people crashed and died; it was never going to happen to me.

Later, when I was stationed at New Castle Army Air Base in Wilmington, Delaware, another accident hit closer to home. I had been ordered to report to Brownsville, Texas, for Pursuit training. Pursuits were fighter planes, far faster with trickier flying characteristics and less forgiving traits than our trainers. One day while practicing formation flying in AT-6's, two of the planes in the formation next to mine touched wings and crashed, killing two girls and an instructor. This time I knew the people involved. Soon after the crash, the class was given R & R, after which we were to report back to Brownsville. Instead of returning to Texas, however, we received telegrams ordering us back to New Castle. I never understood if it was because the Army thought we were too shaken by the accident to continue Pursuit Training, or if it was simply the fact that the war was winding down. At any rate, I never got to fly a Pursuit, something I have always regretted.

In all, thirty-eight women pilots lost their lives during the WASP program. Each time a WASP was killed, it was a reminder to us of our status in the eyes of the military. WASPs did not receive any death benefits and, in fact, had to sign a release discharging the government of any claims, demands or actions on account of death or injury. When a girl died, we had to "pass the hat" to cover the expenses of shipping her body home. The survivors were never compensated by the U.S. government. The coffin could not be covered by an American flag and the family of a WASP killed in the line of duty could not even display the gold star in their window, indicating the loss of a family member to the war.

When the WAFS and WFTD joined to become the WASP, Jackie Cochran was appointed Director of Women Pilots. Not until years later did I become aware of the controversy surrounding her appointment. I know only that I remain grateful to her for the opportunity she gave me. She was someone I looked up to. I was in awe of Jackie Cochran as I was in awe of everything involving the WASP.

September 1943. Graduation. I cannot explain the thrill I experienced when Jackie Cochran pinned the silver WASP wings onto my uniform, wings that proved that not only could girls be pilots; they could fly Army airplanes! Not long ago while participating in a parade in Fort Wayne, Indiana, someone told me how much a collector would give me for those wings. But I wouldn't part with them for any amount of money. To me they are priceless. The wings, which were a redesigned version of the Air Corps pilots' wings, bore our class designation and "319th." The small diamond shape in the center earned us the nickname "flying finance officers." Graduates of 43 W-1 through 43 W-7 received our wings as a gift from

Jackie. It was not until the eighth class of 1943 that the official lozenge adorned the WASP wings.

Following graduation, we were given our choice of assignments. Long Beach, California, I decided, was too far from home. Gene Garvin, who had gone all the way through training with me, chose Romulus, Michigan, but that was too close to home. Dallas was out; I'd had enough of the Texas heat. I finally chose New Castle Army Air Base in Wilmington, Delaware. First, however, I had two weeks leave during which I went home for my sister Violet's wedding. She had achieved her goal of soloing, but after she met Walter Davis, she never had any other interest in flying. At the end of my leave, I reported to the Second Ferrying Division, Air Transport Command in Wilmington — at my own expense.

> *"The girls got in there and plugged harder than the boys. They observe rules, don't zoom or buzz towns. They are as good as men, except for physical strength. For cross country flying you can't beat them."*
> —Elmer Riley, Flight Director, Avenger Field

Wilmington

Someone once suggested that the WASPs were rich girls on a lark. Not true. There was nothing glamorous about it. In my case, I would get orders to go somewhere to pick up an airplane. I would grab my B-4 bag, which was always packed, and my parachute bag, catch a train or get on a commercial flight. When I arrived, I would go to Operations, pick up the airplane and deliver it to its destination. Most of what I flew were trainers and twin-engine troop transports. When trainers needed to be moved from base to base for whatever reason, it was a ferry pilot who did it.

The PT-19's and 26's were made in Hagerstown, Maryland, so I worked out of the

Fairchild factory a lot. It might seem enviable to fly a brand-new airplane right out of the factory, but the negative side was that there could be imperfections in the plane that wouldn't show up until it was in the air. I also flew a lot of Pipers from Lockhaven and got considerable time in the twin Beech. I got my first instrument ticket on a C-47, a twin-engine transport for troops or cargo. Quite often, I worked out of Wichita, where I would pick up a C-45 transport and deliver it to California. After delivery, I would head back to Wichita where another plane would be waiting to be taken to California or perhaps in the opposite direction to Buffalo, New York.

When any of us made a delivery, our orders were to return to home base or back to the factory by the quickest means possible. We were not allowed to fly after sunset, so if a mission could not be completed by then, we had to land at a designated air field, send an RON (Remain Over Night), and find a place to stay in a hotel or maybe nurses' quarters on the base. The next day we would be off by daybreak. When I was lucky, I could get a flight on a commercial airline. I carried a pass that gave me priority on flights, permitting me to "bump" anyone except the President. Often, though, the only way back was by train. If there was no seat available, I would throw my bags down in the little space between cars and go to sleep. Glamorous? Hardly.

Sometimes the men at the Army airfields were surprised to see a woman climb out of a plane. The Army had not publicized our presence, so often the men did not even know there were women fliers until one of us landed in their midst. There were, interestingly enough, those commanding officers who actually preferred WASPs to male ferry pilots. We had a reputation for being dedicated to our jobs and delivering planes quickly. There were no days off in the Ferrying Division; I wouldn't have taken them if there were. I didn't want to miss a chance to fly.

The ease with which I adapted to the ferry pilot's lifestyle I probably owe to my parents. When I was young, I remember, my parents took us on a trip to the Chicago World's Fair. We drove to Chicago from Fort Wayne, saw the Fair, and drove back all in one day, a considerable distance for the 1930's. Another time, they decided to take us to see Niagara Falls. Money was tight, but they didn't let that stop them. Because there were no coolers then, Mother packed peanut butter and things that would travel well so that we would not have to eat in restaurants. There weren't motels as there are now, so when my dad wasn't able to find a reasonably priced room for us, he just pulled off on a side street and the five of us went to sleep in the car. Sometime in the middle of the night a policeman tapped on the window, inquiring if there was a problem.

"No," Dad assured him. "We just came up to see the Falls and didn't have a place to stay. We're just taking a little nap so we'll be ready to start home in the morning." By the time I joined the Ferry Division, I was an old hand at sleeping in cars. Sleeping between train cars wasn't all that different. At any rate, I wasn't afraid to do it.

Many of the original WAFS pilots, an elite squadron of highly qualified women under the command of Nancy Love, were at Wilmington.

When I got there, of course, I was one of Jackie Cochran's girls. There was some tension between the two groups due to controversy regarding the choice of Jackie over Nancy Love as Director of Women Pilots' Training, but generally the other women treated me well. At one Powder Puff race years later, I was talking to Betty Gillies, who was one of the original WAFS. "I never got to go anywhere but Wilmington," I complained, still bemoaning the fact that I had not had the opportunity to fly pursuits.

"You never got to go anywhere?" she answered. "Maybe they kept you because you were a good pilot." I hadn't thought of it that way, but still I wished I had pushed for a chance to fly pursuits. Back in 1943, of course, I was just so glad to be doing what I was doing that I flew whatever they gave me without question.

BOQ 14, a two-story barracks similar to Army officers' quarters, was my home in Wilmington. I had my own room for which I paid fifteen to twenty dollars a month. I especially remember the wooden floors that constantly snagged my stockings! We were allowed to use the Officers' Club and buy our meals at the Officers' Mess. By November of 1943, we finally had an official WASP uniform — Santiago Blues. We wore the ATC buttons on our shoulders and our WASP wings. Enlisted men gave us salutes, but technically we were civilians with civil service status. Our pay, two hundred fifty dollars a month plus six dollars a day when we were away from base on assignment, was slightly less than a second lieutenant's with flight pay. We did not have a rank so there was no promotion or increase in pay based on how long a girl had been in the service. There was a ready room in the front of the barracks. Every morning we would check the bulletin board to see if we had a trip out. If not, we would be listed to go over to the Link or another training session on meteorology, navigation, or new flying techniques. Just because there was no trip did not mean we got free time.

There wasn't much time for a personal life. I did have dinner a few times with one nice guy, a Lt. Dickens, but it was difficult to see him when we were both out on trips. It was against regulations for men and women to be on the same flights, but it did happen occasionally. Developing close friendships with other girls was just as difficult. It was possible that out of six weeks, a pilot might spend only a few nights at home base. I would get a trip with someone and we would be out for two or three weeks. We would enjoy each other's company, but then on the next trip I would be assigned to someone else.

During one period of time I shared several trips with a girl named Joanne Wallace. Josie had a car and, better yet, rationing stamps for gas. Whenever she went out on a trip, she would leave her car keys for me. I don't recall that I ever got the chance to drive the car, but I thought it was nice of her to offer. We became friends. She was engaged, and I remember the gifts she got from her fiancé, Bob Orr, who later became the governor of Indiana. I even had plans to be in her wedding. Her mother was going to get my measurements and have my dress made, but in the end I was denied permission to leave, even though it was only days before the WASP was to be disbanded.

Years later in Chicago on a trip, I was talking to some pilots from Indianapolis. When they mentioned they were flying the Governor, I said, " Oh, when he comes back, tell him Margaret from Fort Wayne says 'Hello.'" They looked at me as if to say, "Sure, lady, we bet the Governor knows who you are." Later we were in an upstairs pilots' lounge and when it was about time for our customers to come, we walked down to the waiting room together. A few minutes later, Bob Orr came in, took one look at me and said, "Maggie! What are you doing here?" As I greeted him, I couldn't help but glance over at the two dumbfounded pilots. So. . . the Governor wouldn't know me?

✈

I Fell Off the Roof

It was a generally held belief that women were handicapped during their monthly cycles and would need to be off duty for a few days each month. We were thought to be unreliable because of this theory. Jackie Cochran wanted to prove that it was not true so we became guinea pigs of a sort. Every month when a WASP had her period, she had to report to the medical officer, " I fell off the roof." That was what we had to say! It was an embarrassment for many of us. If we were slated for a flight test, moreover, we could choose to postpone it until after "that time of the month" because the Army thought we wouldn't be up to par. Looking back, it was all pretty silly, considering that only a few years later, when expecting my first child, I managed to squeeze myself into a cockpit until I barely had room to pull the stick back. Obviously, the fears that women could not handle the rigors of flying for the military proved to be unfounded. Even cases of fatigue among women pilots were rare. Maybe it was because we wanted to fly so badly and prove that we were as good as the men that we just refused to give in to fatigue, or maybe we were just too stubborn to admit that we might be tired.

Although there are still those who have complaints about bias against women in the military, for the most part I felt that the men treated me quite well. Occasionally when guys were about to be shipped overseas, we would hear comments like, "Why don't you go back to riveting in the factory where you're really needed?" They resented the fact that they were being sent into combat because we were there to take over the ferrying jobs. Another was, "Why are you here anyway?" I heard that comment more than once, but I tried not to take it personally. After all, they were going into combat and they had a right to be scared.

Because there were some men who thought we couldn't pull our own weight, we constantly had to prove ourselves. I remember one time a few of us girls had gone over to the Officers' Mess to eat. The tables were long with benches and everyone just squeezed in wherever there was room. We were talking about what we wanted to do later that evening and someone suggested roller skating. A couple of the male officers overheard and said, "That sounds like fun. How many are going?" About that time, the fellow sitting next to me passed the dessert, which was a large tray of fruit. He held it out and, thinking he was going to hold it for me, I reached out to take some grapes.

"If you can fly airplanes, you can hold your own tray," he said, and let go, spilling the entire contents in my lap. My face burned with embarrassment. All the time we were eating, he hadn't even spoken to anyone. I couldn't imagine why he was so angry at me. From this and other such incidents I came to understand that male pilots, especially fighter pilots, liked to flaunt their bravado in front of non-fliers and brag about their prowess in an airplane. It probably wounded their egos to have anyone see a hundred-pound girl climb out of a plane. It made the men look bad. Later at the skating rink, he came over to me and apologized. I guess when he spilled the fruit in my lap, all his anger spilled out too, and he never gave me anymore trouble. My approach to dealing with hostility after that was to ignore it and do my job. Usually that was all it took.

> "*The WASP, according to medical surveys, had as much endurance and were no more subject to fatigue and flew as regularly and for as long hours as the male pilots in similar work. . . the conclusion of the medical studies is, 'It is no longer a matter of speculation that graduate WASPs were adapted physically, mentally, and psychologically to the type of flying assigned.'"*
> —Jacqueline Cochran in Report on the Women's Pilot Program

One rule that worked against many of my sex was the height requirement. I could not fly four-engine planes because I was too short. At five feet four inches, I was two inches shy of the height requirement. I was able to get some time in the big C-54's and B-24 Liberators as copilot, however. Both were large (for that time) four-engine aircraft — C-54's for hauling cargo and the B-24's for toting bomb loads. My first 24 ride was quite an experience. I had just delivered a plane somewhere in the South and was looking for a ride back to Wilmington. When I asked, the office manager said, "Oh, good. We have a 24 that just came in from the Pacific." The pilot had dismissed his crew and the airplane needed to go up to Washington immediately. " We have a pilot and engineer, but we need a copilot. Are you interested?"

Of course I was interested! I couldn't wait to get my hands on that big bomber. I handed him my black checkout book and he sent me out to familiarize myself with the airplane while they rounded up the crew. I was sitting in the cockpit, checking things out, when the pilot arrived. He didn't conceal his shock. " What are you doing?" he demanded.

"I'm to be your copilot, Sir," I replied. He was visibly annoyed. I think he thought someone was trying to pull a trick on him by sending a young woman out to sit in his plane. My name had been posted on the board as "MJ Ray." The pilot had been in such a hurry that when he glanced at the assignment he had taken it to be Major Ray. No one told him before he came out to the plane that I was a WASP. In fact, he hadn't even known there were any women pilots. Once again, I realized how well the military was keeping our "secret." He got in the plane and we just sat there. Finally he looked at me and said, "If you know so much, start it up." Using the checklist, I did it, but it was a slow start. I tried to taxi it around, but couldn't do it alone because steering the large plane on the ground was done with a big wheel instead of the rudder I was used to. I guess the fact that I had tried, though, was enough. He didn't say any more and I sensed from that moment on that we were no longer adversaries.

Another time I happened into a chance to fly a C-45. I had an order to pick up an L-6 trainer known as a Colver Cadet. When I got to Wichita, I mentioned to the captain there, whose last name, by the way, was Ray, that I didn't particularly like Colver Cadets. " We need a pilot for a C-45," he said. "Ever flown one?" At that time I had not and I told him so. "I'll tell you what," he said. "I'm not supposed to take the time to check anyone out, but if you can check out in one circuit around the field, I'll put you on board." I wasn't going to refuse a chance like that. We took it out, went once around the field and landed. Shortly after that I was on my way back East to Niagara piloting the C-45 twin-engine transport. I guess I did a good job because they sent me right back for another one and then another. It was nearly a month before I got back to home base.

> *"Half the battle around here is to show the men we can do it. We're not tomboys either. We're proud of being feminine."*—Joanne Garrett, WASP trainee

✈

I'll Not Be Home For Christmas

With Christmas of 1943 approaching, a wave of longing swept over me every time I heard the strains of " I'll Be Home for Christmas" on the radio. I loved the travel involved in my job as a WASP, and most of the time I was too busy to be homesick. I had learned to enjoy the people and holidays wherever I happened to be. Easter, the Fourth of July, even Thanksgiving, had passed without a problem; but Christmas, I discovered, was a different story. I hadn't realized how being away from my family at Christmas was going to affect me. Although resigned to the situation, I was depressed for the first time since leaving home. Be realistic, I told myself. There are thousands of service people. The war can't be put on hold while we all go home for the holidays.

On December 23, orders came in for four PT-26's, the Canadian version of the PT-19's with canopy-enclosed cockpits, to be ferried from Hagerstown, Maryland, to Winnipeg, Canada. I drew the assignment along with the flight commander, Nancy Baker, Jill McCormick, and a third WASP. At least I would be busy on Christmas instead of moping around the base feeling sorry for myself. Then I found out we would be taking a refueling stop in Fort Wayne. I kept my elation to myself until we landed at Baer Field. "Couldn't we stop just for the night?" I begged Nancy, explaining that this was my home. In true military fashion, she reminded me that we were on duty and that we were under orders to complete the mission without delay. Knowing she was right, however, didn't make it any easier to swallow.

"We have about fifteen minutes to refuel and get on our way," Nancy told us. "The weather is closing in fast and I want to get to South Bend yet tonight." Fifteen minutes. Hardly enough time to borrow a car and drive out to the farm. I longed at least to pick up a phone and wish my parents "Merry Christmas," but there was no phone at the farmhouse. Ironically, being so close to them made my family seem even farther away.

In a matter of minutes we were fueled up and ready to go. The lineman came out to hand crank the planes. Mine started without a hitch, then Nancy's, then the third girl's, but every time Jill got hers started, it would sputter and die. The lineman tried again and again to crank the plane, even using the primer on the outside, but the airplane would not start. Nancy, irritated by the delay, shut down her own plane and ran over to see what was going on. She climbed up on the wing of Jill's plane and watched as she tried again to start it. I could see her yelling at Jill, demanding that she try again. Even with Nancy's instructions, Jill and the lineman just could not keep the engine running. Nancy motioned for the rest of us to shut down our engines. The weather had closed in on us and we were stuck in Fort Wayne!

Trying to hide my glee, I called a friend to get us a ride to the farm. My mother, not knowing I was in Indiana, was overjoyed to see us. She did her best to pamper and feed us all. Funny thing, though, how that plane started right up on the first try the day after Christmas. I knew that Jill, with the help of the lineman, had somehow managed to hex the plane, but it couldn't have been easy with Nancy standing right over them. I didn't even know the lineman's name so I never had the opportunity to thank him, but years later I found a way to pay my debt to Jill — and in the best way imaginable.

I had been doing some work in Sturgis, Michigan, instructing and checking people out on planes for George Bailey, who had an airplane dealership there. When it came time for the Southern Michigan All Lady Lark (S.M.A.L.L.) race, it was natural that I ask him for a plane to fly in the race. After all, it would be good advertising for him too. Then for some reason, he offered a second plane, asking if I knew anyone else who would want to fly the race. I immediately called Jill, who was working at Purdue University, only a few hours away. She jumped at the chance. George, not knowing Jill's credentials on the Bonanza, insisted on being her copilot. My copilot, the mayor of Sturgis, showed up with a road map! But, we had fun and I was able to thank Jill for the Christmas of 1943 in a most appropriate way — a chance to fly.

I'm Coming Straight In!

If flying a brand-new plane straight out of the factory had its risks, flying an old, worn-out plane was definitely an adventure. One time I had a trip in a UC-78. I was to fly the twin-engine Cessna, known in the Ferry Division as the Bamboo Bomber, to Montgomery, Alabama, to be scrapped. I was alone in the plane when just past Washington, DC, the plane developed a serious vibration. I shut down one engine to see if that would get rid of it. When that didn't work, I tried the other engine. Finally I got on the radio and contacted the nearest tower. " I have vibration," I reported.

"What is your name, rank, and serial number?" the voice on the radio asked. I told him. Then he asked me about the panel, what the air speed was, what the different temperatures were. When he started asking ridiculous questions like, "Where were you born?" and "What's your family like?" I realized that he was trying to distract me so I wouldn't panic. Actually, I was quite calm, probably because I didn't yet feel that I was in an emergency situation. Finally, when I was over a sparsely populated area, he told me the plane was not worth saving and that I should abandon the aircraft and jump. I got out of my seat and started to the back of the plane, but maneuvering between the seats to get to the door on the left side seemed like too much trouble. Besides, I didn't want to jump. It wasn't that I was scared; it just didn't seem necessary. I went back to the microphone. "I still have control of the airplane," I told him. "I'm going to stay with it. I think I can make Winston-Salem." A short time later I reported, "I have the airport in sight."

"Switch over to tower," came the voice on the radio, giving me the tower frequency.

"This is Army two-four-six, straight in for 23," I called.

The tower came back: "We observe left-hand pattern only." Are they crazy? I thought. I was losing altitude; I didn't have enough to go around the airport and come back in. At that point, I didn't care if they liked it or not; I was going straight in. A moment later I heard, "Two-four-six. Two-four-six. You're the aircraft in distress. The field has been cleared for you." Just over the fence, I dropped my gear. I thought the landing went pretty well until I looked out and saw raw gas running over the left engine. I hadn't noticed it when the throttle was forward and the airplane was going faster. Then I spotted the fire truck and the ambulance and a whole string of equipment coming out to meet me. I tried to stand up and get out, but the prop was still windmilling. When I saw the fire hoses pointed straight at me, I knew that if there was a flash of fire when I opened the door, the pressure from the hoses would blow me right back into the airplane. I reached up and closed everything down and hustled out of the plane.

The commanding officer, who had come out as soon as he heard there was a problem, commended me for bringing the aircraft down safely and offered me a ride back in the staff car. He assured me they would take care of towing the airplane in. As soon as I got inside, I had to call my home base. I told the safety officer back at Wilmington that I'd had a forced landing, but I had set it down with no damage to the plane except for the blown engine. He exploded. "How can there be no damage to the undercarriage if you had the gear up?" he demanded.

"I put the gear down, Sir," I replied. Now according to regulations, emergency landings were all done with gear up. The theory is that the pilot can slide the plane in better and stop more quickly. Up to that point I had been calm and in control of the situation, but when he started to curse, I lost it. The commanding officer was standing close by watching me, and I turned my back to him so he wouldn't see my tears. The next thing I knew, he took the phone and got an earful of what was intended for me.

"What's your name, rank, and serial number?" he demanded of the voice at the other end. I thought that was the end of it until two weeks later when I was assigned to take someone down to a point of embarkation in another airplane. I nearly fainted when I realized it was the same captain who had given me a piece of his mind on the telephone. He was being shipped overseas. I picked him up in Wilmington in a twin Beech and headed for Savannah. About halfway down, I noticed that the oil temperature had gone "in the red." I was afraid we were going to have a serious problem. "I don't want to blow an engine," I told my passenger. "I'm going to have to shut it down." It became obvious that he wasn't very happy about it. It was getting on toward nightfall and he started asking nervous questions about how much night flying I had done. I didn't want to declare an emergency so I asked him to get me the tower frequency. When I realized how agitated he was though, I decided to do it myself. We made it to the base and did a single-engine landing. He jumped out of the plane and stalked off without so much as a "thank you for the ride" or anything! I never saw him again. Actually I did feel a little sorry for him. He was being shipped overseas, hopefully not for what he had said on the phone, and I had scared him half to death before he even got there.

I made another unscheduled landing in Ohio one time. Aware that there was weather coming in, I got an early start, flying out of Bradley Field in Connecticut at sunrise. Headed west, I stopped in Pittsburgh to refuel. Fort Wayne was to be my next stop because there was a military field there. Coming across Ohio, I began to relax, feeling comfortable with the familiar, square fields. Since I was so close to home, I wasn't following the map as closely as I should have. Suddenly I realized I was lost.

Back then our radio communication consisted of Morse code "dits" and "dahs," but my headset was getting too much static for me to follow it. With the weather moving in on me, I went down and circled the town, trying in vain to locate a name that was on my map. Then I spotted a farmer out plowing his field. I went down and flew the length of the field. When I had checked it out, I dropped my gear, came in and landed. Imagine his surprise when I jumped out of the plane and started running toward him. All of a sudden, it was as if people had stepped out of the fence posts. They were all pointing at me. "Look, a girl! Flying a B-25!" I had to laugh. Military planes usually had big numbers on the sides of them and this plane had come from Bradley Field so it had a "B" on it and the number 25. To the uninitiated, I guess that made it a B-25. Anyway, I found out I was close to Defiance, Ohio. Knowing there was a nearby railroad track running into Fort Wayne, I jumped back in the plane, took off again and followed the tracks the rest of the way. Since the tracks ran just a little over a mile from my parents' farm, I couldn't resist the urge to circle the house before heading to Baer Field. When I realized at the airport that I was going to be weathered in for a few days, I sat down to wait. I was sure my folks would know it had been me over the house and come to the airport to meet me. When they didn't come, I called a friend, Johnny Amstutz, to take me out to the farm. My parents were completely surprised. "Didn't you hear me fly over the house?" I asked.

"We heard the plane go over and went out to look," my mother said. "But I never dreamed my little Margaret Jane could fly anything that big or that fast." Enjoying all the attention, I never dreamed that it would all come to an end soon after that.

ANOTHER VOICE:

Jackie Cochran
(IN A LETTER TO ALL WASP)

"The Army Air Force will issue a certificate of honorable service and discharge similar to the type issued to officers when they are relieved from active duty. In addition, you will receive a card designating you as a rated pilot of military aircraft indicating the horsepower rating for which you are qualified. This card can be used as a basis to obtain a CAA Commercial license in the same manner as do military male pilots. . .Those who wish to continue to fly for the Army Air Force will be disappointed, but no WASP familiar with the pertinent facts would question the decision or its time limits. . ."

General H.H. Arnold
(IN A LETTER TO ALL WASP)

"The WASP became part of the Army Air Forces. . .in order to release male pilots for other duties. Their very successful record of accomplishments has proved that in any future total effort the nation can count on thousands of its young women to fly any of its aircraft. You have freed male pilots for other work, but now the war situation has changed and the time has come when your volunteered services are no longer needed. The situation is that, if you continue in service, you will be replacing instead of releasing our young men. I know that the WASP wouldn't want that. So I have directed that the WASP program be inactivated and all WASP be released on 20 December 1944."

By December 1944, 1074 WASP had graduated from training. They had flown over 60,000,000 miles averaging 33 hours per month. Women in the Ferrying Division had flown 78 types of aircraft from trainers to pursuits, transports, cargo ships, and bombers, including the B-29 Superfortress. Thirty-eight women had died in service to their country. Early in the Spring of 1945, WASP histories and reports were filed in government archives as classified information. For the time being, the AAF forgot women had ever been in the cockpit.

✈

Women Need Not Apply

After we got the notification that the WASP was being deactivated, there was a mad scramble of girls trying to find a way to continue flying. We even tried to get the Air Force to hire us for one dollar a year plus expenses. General Arnold was in favor of keeping women pilots active in some capacity, but he could not justify it unless we were militarized. There had been talk of militarization, but at the time most of us were too busy to give it much thought. I don't even recall hearing any gossip about it at the time, and it was not until years later that I found out the details in a book about the WASP. Militarization would have given us benefits, but it also would have meant that we could not quit if we wanted to. Of course, quitting was never on my mind, but there were those who had quit to get married or had simply taken the training and gone home.

When early in 1944 it seemed that militarization was likely, I was sent to AAF Tactical School in Orlando, Florida, for a three week course designed to prepare me to become an officer. Then in June 1944, a bill to militarize women pilots went to Congress and was defeated, mostly due to strong lobbying by male civilian flight instructors attached to the Army. With the war winding down, it wasn't necessary for the AAF to continue its wartime pilot training program. All civilian flight instructors would then be out of their high paying jobs and eligible for the draft. They wanted the ferrying jobs that we had and were afraid that we would get priority if we were militarized.

The letter from Jackie Cochran in October 1944 came as quite a shock. I was crushed. How could it be over? Since we had originally been hired as civilian pilots, Ferrying Division Headquarters suggested that we simply be rehired. We argued that if we were discharged, it should at least be a gradual process. Shortly after, however, General Arnold sent a memo to all Air Force commands. Other than Jackie Cochran, there would be no women pilots in any capacity in the Air Force after December 20. In fact, the only place we could have continued to fly was England, since women were still ferrying airplanes across the English Channel in January 1945.

A committee was formed to investigate the possibility of the WASP being absorbed into the Women's Army Corps (WAC), where we would be commissioned as Rated Flying Officers. There were many arguments both for and against this move, but in the end it never came to pass. We remained a civilian volunteer organization in the eyes of the Army until our deactivation and as such were not entitled to veteran's benefits. We received no hospitalization, no death benefits. We were not entitled to education or housing assistance under the G.I. Bill. All official Army insignia had to be removed from our uniforms as of midnight December 20, 1944, after which time only WASP wings could be worn with the Santiago Blues. We were allowed to keep one complete uniform and a set of insignia. As promised, we were issued a certificate of service along with our pilot qualifications. I left the WASP with a First Lieutenant commission, having signed up for the Army Air Force Reserve.

The most difficult prospect for most of us was the possibility that we would never fly again. After the war, places were just not interested in hiring women for flying jobs. After all, there were all those male pilots coming home who needed the work. The Army Air Force gave us references to help us in our job searches, but they recommended us for "civilian, clerical, professional, or technical ground positions." And did we have offers! There was an opening for secretary to the Air Traffic Control Board or better still, secretary to the manager of Aviation Gas Sales. Had I ever gotten around to nurse's training, there were openings for Air Evacuation nurses. Even the Civil Aeronautics Authority offered jobs to former WASPs doing "communication work."

The response to our applications was always the same. "We do not have any pilot position open, and I do not anticipate any at this field; however, I do have an opening as Control Tower Operator and another as dispatcher. The salary for these positions is $100 to $175 a month." Jackie had approached Riddle Mackay Aero College in Clewiston, Florida, about the possibility of hiring women as Link instructors. The answer? "Prior to this time we had not considered putting girls in the Link department and some thought must be given to this problem. If any of the girls care to make applications for this work, they may do so, and I will advise them of our policy at that time." Boeing was accepting applications from women for test pilot jobs, but applicants needed a degree in engineering. When I was offered a job as a stewardess for a foreign airline, I couldn't help but wonder how many male pilots would have accepted a job like that after the war. Still I might have taken the job if my parents hadn't been pushing for me to stay home for awhile.

Several of us got jobs flying out to Arizona to pick up planes from the "boneyard" where the military stored used planes, and ferrying them back to Michigan. I had four or five trips the spring after I got out of the service, but the planes were in pretty bad shape. Surprisingly, I never had a forced landing in any of them, but the fabric did pop off a few.

During that winter, when Pierce Flying Service needed an airplane picked up in Buffalo, New York, I jumped at the chance to go get it. When I got there the weather was bad with snow piled almost as high as the wings on the Taylorcraft L-2. I had to wait for snowplows to clear the runway before I could get out. On the way home, I realized that the gas gauge was going down too fast. By the time I got as far as Erie, Pennsylvania, I knew I was going to have to land. Circling the airport, I could see that the runways were all covered with snow, but when I'm nearly out of gas, I land the airplane, snow or no snow! I circled again. I could just make out the runway. There were cars parked at the hangar, so I knew there was someone there, and in I came. The snow was deeper than I anticipated, but I taxied it in. A quick check showed that the tank was leaking, but I didn't want to get stranded in Erie, so I had them fill it up anyway. Someone ran a truck down the runway to clear a space for me to take off as others helpfully pointed out that I would never get it off the ground. About a year later, I met a mechanic out at Smith Field in Fort Wayne. "I made ten dollars on you once," he said.

"How's that?"

"I was at the airport in Erie the day you took off in all that snow. Everyone was saying you wouldn't get it off the ground, but I said, 'If she can land it, I'll bet she can get it out.'" He was right.

In February 1945 I sent a letter to the CAA asking for an interview in regards to an air-marking job that involved flying to a location and painting directional markings on top of buildings. With confidence, I listed my qualifications. I had completed ground school at Indiana Technical College and was a graduate of WASP training. I had a valid commercial pilot certificate for 0-1350-horsepower, single and twin-engine ratings and about 1800 hours of flying time, much of which was cross country. I got a prompt reply. "We regret that at the present time we have no opening for a person of your special qualifications, but should we have a vacancy later, we should be very pleased to give you consideration along with other applicants." I never heard from them again. Soon after that I went to California on the train to visit my friend, Dorothy Amstutz. I had my instructor's rating and a job at Pierce by that time, but I was getting tired of sitting around waiting for students. A ferry pilot's heart beat within me. I needed to go somewhere. Anywhere.

"It would seem that a woman's success in any particular line would prove her fitness for that work, without regard to theories to the contrary."—Ruth Law in Air Travel

Ready to go flying at Smith Field 1942

Ready for a training session in the PT-19A. Quite a change from the J-3 Cub I had been flying back in Fort Wayne!

*With my baymates at Sweetwater (front to back):
Sylvia Dahme, Maggie Ray, Wilma Morehead, Sylvia
Schwartz, Fran Greene, Eugenia (Gene) Garvin*

*The Dickens brothers. I remember Louis (on the right) who
was supposed to be my date to the WASP Farewell Dinner.
Oddly enough, I don't recall the name of the brother (in the
middle) who took his place.*

*Taking time out from flying at Avenger Field (1943) to pose
in my glamourous "zoot" suit.*

My baymates: (l to r in back) Me, Wilma Morehead, Fran Greene, Sylvia Dahme. (kneeling) Gene Garvin and Sylvia Schwartz.

Posing at Sweetwater before a flying session.

In the cockpit, ready to log some hours in the air.

In my Santiago Blues--official WASP uniform --while stationed at New Castle Army Air Base in Wilmington, Delaware

Wings of Margaret Ray Ringenberg earned from 1942-1944

Civil Air Patrol Wings received in Ft. Wayne 1942

Class 43-W5 received at Avenger Field Sweetwater, Texas Sept. 1943

Official lozenge issued later at New Castle Army Air Base

Air Transport Command Civilian Pilot Wings received 2nd Ferrying Division, NCAAB, Wilmington, Delaware

Air Force insignia from uniform 1943

Air Transport Command insignia 1943

W.A.S.P. insignia from uniform 1943

In my WASP uniform complete with black purse, ready to fly a ferry trip out of New Castle Army Air Base.

1946- The new Mr. and Mrs. Morris Ringenberg on our wedding day with Morris's father, Rev. J.A. Ringenberg.

PART THREE

Mixing Flying and Family

"(What the girls want after the war). . .husbands and babies. I've told them, and they know it to be true, that there'll be no place for them in the military or commercial aviation when the world's at peace again. After victory, they'll be wives first and aviation fans second -- the sort of women who've done a lot to make America what it is today." -- Jackie Cochran in the <u>Sweetwater Reporter,</u> May 5, 1943

✈

After the WASP, What?

The trip home from Wilmington on the train could not have been more depressing. I had never before experienced such a total feeling of dejection. Looking back, I should have realized that the end was near. More and more frequently my trips had been limited to moving military personnel and delivering planes to the scrapyard. It had been months since I had gone to Fairchild or Cessna or Piper to test and ferry new airplanes.

The last few days at New Castle had seemed unreal as I scrambled around, shipping boxes home, returning my parachute, my leather suit and other equipment to flight operations. The farewell dinner, a long dress affair, had been a disappointment as well. The flight officer who had asked to be my escort was called out on a trip at the last minute, and it was his brother, a first lieutenant, who showed up at my door with a flower. I would gladly have missed the dinner for a chance to fly one more trip.

Now here I was, sad and depressed, on a noisy, dirty train, headed for home. But to what? The farmhouse I loved had been replaced by a house in the city. My furniture had been moved into a new bedroom for my homecoming, but it was not my room with the familiar view of red barn and fields.

When the excitement of seeing my family had worn off, I realized that more than just my address had changed. The young men I had known were still overseas, and many of my girlfriends had married and moved to be closer to their husbands. Life in Fort Wayne just didn't measure up to the excitement of the WASP experience. I drove out to Smith Field just to check things out. As I pulled into the airport, I saw it — 35735, the number on the little yellow Cub I had soloed. Not everything had changed. The hangars and the runway were still there, still the same. I began to fall into the familiar pattern of hanging around the airport again.

ANOTHER VOICE:

Fred Bunyan
(FORMER OWNER, PIERCE FLYING SERVICE)

After the war all my money was in a safe deposit box in Fort Wayne in the form of savings bonds. I also had some money coming to me from war bonds, but there was a shortage of cash. Margaret lent me the final two thousand dollars I needed to buy Pierce Flying Service which consisted of eighteen planes. Then, after Margaret earned her instructor's license, she worked for the service. People could rent the planes to use for lessons just as anyone else would rent a car from an agency. If someone came out to rent a plane and we didn't know him, Margaret would take him up and let him fly around a little and shoot a couple of landings just to make sure he knew what he was doing before we let him have the plane.

Because of my experience in the military, I was one of the first pilots in Fort Wayne to get a multi-engine rating. Then, in March 1945 I got my instructor's rating and began working for Pierce Flying Service. Right off, I discovered that male students did not want to fly with me unless there wasn't any other instructor available. They seemed to think it took some kind of superman to fly an airplane and, in their eyes, I didn't qualify. It was frustrating, but I handled the situation by being patient and waiting for opportunities. For awhile the CAA seemed to take a closer look at female pilots. Even with my military experience, it still seemed I had to prove myself in what was considered a man's profession, but in the end it forced me to be sharper and work harder to succeed. Recently, after recounting this story at a speaking engagement, a man approached me. "I should know you," I said. He introduced himself. He had been a teenager when I started instructing, but he had been taking lessons from a rival flight service.

"We weren't prejudiced, Margaret," he explained. "We were just shy because you were so pretty. In fact when the other guys and I saw you, we said, 'Men, we're taking lessons at the wrong place!'"

A few months after I began instructing, someone from WGL radio called the flying service and said, "We have some pamphlets put together to announce when Japan surrenders. We want to be the first in the air to distribute them when the time comes." These were to be scattered by plane to help spread the joyful news of V-J Day. Before long, the phone rang again and it was someone from WOWO radio with a similar proposal. We had to tell them we were already committed. "We'll get someone else," they said, and I was all the more determined to be the first in the air to make the drop.

The pamphlets were delivered to the airport and we loaded them into two J-3 Cubs. We stayed at the airport for two days, waiting. It was mid-afternoon on August 14, 1945 when the call came in. We had the planes ready and a helper lined up to ride along in each and throw out the papers. The CAA had given us clearance to make the drop and they hadn't specified how high I had to fly, so I went right through downtown Fort Wayne, down Calhoun Street and over the parking lots of several factories, peppering the sky with the good news that the war was over. When people came out of work that day, they saw, lying everywhere, papers announcing:

JAPAN SURRENDERS.

Such a historic moment warranted front

page headlines, but there was no front page. Both newspapers in town were on strike. The only time I ever "buzzed" downtown Fort Wayne, and I didn't even get my picture in the paper! But what a thrill for this Indiana farm girl not only to have served her country in its time of need, but then get to deliver the good news when the war ended! In 1995, the fiftieth anniversary of the surrender, I happened to hear someone on WGL talk radio mention the dropping of the flyers, adding, "If anyone has information about the pilot of that plane, please call." I immediately dialed the station and proclaimed, "That was me!" And as frosting on the cake, I got to do the drop all over again on the anniversary. This time I stayed out of downtown.

Basically, I'm just the lady next door. I don't think about whether I'm making history. I just love to fly.
— Margaret Ringenberg

✈

WASP Stings Timberwolf

While I was stationed at Wilmington in 1943 I received a copy of my church's bulletin with the names and addresses of all the service people from the congregation. I exchanged letters with many of them, including a boy from home named Morris Ringenberg. His sister, Lois, and I were friends and I remembered him from church. One time I was scheduled to go to Hagerstown, Maryland, with two other WASPs to pick up a plane from the Fairchild factory, but before we even got out of New Castle, there was a problem with our plane. I took advantage of the delay to run to my mailbox, and there was a letter from Morris, telling me that he was stationed at Hagerstown. When we arrived, it was too late to

check out the plane and take care of the paperwork, so we checked into a hotel and called Morris. He came into town and took all three of us to
dinner. It was great fun seeing someone from
home, but I thought of him strictly as a friend, not
a date.

I left the service in December 1944, but it
was not until the summer of 1945 that Morris returned with a Purple Heart, having been wounded
in Germany. When I saw him in church, we would
swap stories of the military and talk about the
difficulty of adjusting to life at home again. Other
people just did not understand. Then at Christmas that year, there was a terrible snowstorm in
Fort Wayne. The streetcars were not running and
I was bored sitting home. I gave Morris a call. He
was disappointed that a trip to Archbold, Ohio, for
Christmas dinner had been canceled because of
the weather. He was sitting home, bored too.
"That's too bad," I said. "Our family is getting together at my sister's house." On an impulse, I
asked him to go along, just as I would have any
Army buddy. My family was, however, a little per-
turbed. Maybe they thought the Christmas gifts
of sheets and other things they had purchased for
my hope chest would make a young man uncomfortable. I thought they were making a big deal
out of nothing. He was just a friend, not a boy-
friend. My family obviously saw something I
didn't.

Shortly after that Christmas, Morris and I
started dating. Around February, Dorothy
Amstutz's mother talked me into taking the train
to California again to persuade Dorothy to come
home. Since Dorothy was already homesick, it

didn't take much convincing. While I was there, Morris sent me a Valentine and by late summer we were engaged. On a trip to the Wisconsin Dells with friends, he gave me my diamond. It was perfect except for one minor detail. It didn't fit.

We were married in October 1946 at the home of Morris's parents. His father, a minister, performed the ceremony. There were no guests other than our parents, my sister Violet, who was my maid of honor, and the best man, Morris's brother, Jess. My parents invited the rest of our families to a dinner at their home in our honor. The Fort Wayne *Journal Gazette* reported the marriage in a column called "Sky Talk."

"Morris, cashier of the Grabill Bank, was a member of the famed Timberwolf 164th Division of Engineers that was first across the Rhine. He first served in the Pacific Theater. Hence, Maggie has been saying that the WASP stung the Timberwolf."

My dad owned an apartment house in the Lakeside area of Fort Wayne and it was there we began our married life. I remember shortly after the wedding I was having a conversation with Dorothy, who had also recently married. In the course of the conversation, it suddenly hit me. That "Mrs." in front of my name changed everything. I was no longer Maggie Ray, pilot; I was Mrs. Morris Ringenberg. It was my first and only identity crisis, but it didn't last long. Morris had known me while I was flying for the military, and I had been flying for Pierce when we started dating. Never once did he ask me to quit. He always accepted my flying as part of the package. "I let Margaret fly," he likes to tell friends, "and she lets me play golf." It's been quite a good arrangement for over fifty years.

Morris Ringenberg
(HUSBAND)

I've known Margaret since she was a little girl. Our parents knew each other and our families attended the same church. The young people from First Missionary Church often went out to the Ray farm for activities—tennis and homemade ice cream. Margaret's older sisters were closer to my age. At sixteen, I suppose I barely noticed ten-year-old Margaret. I certainly never anticipated marrying her back then!

Later when we were both in the service, we corresponded like many of the young people from our church, and once she stopped to see me while on a ferrying trip. So I knew she was a pilot when I married her. I thought it was great and saw nothing wrong with her continuing to fly after we were married. In fact I encouraged her to do it. Flying was her job. It's what she did.

When the kids were little she was working as a flight instructor, but she took good care of the children and always made provisions for them when she had to be gone a few hours. They were not aware that it was anything unusual. When the airstrip was behind our house, she could give a lesson, land and have lunch with them and take off again. She tried to interest me in flying, and together we won the Kentucky Air Derby several times. I was her copilot until they discontinued the race. She taught me what I needed to know in case I had to fly the plane, but I never had any desire to take up flying myself. I like flying with her, but I don't like to miss work. I just tell her someone has to stay home and make a living!

✈

What Does Your Mommy Do?

A couple of months into our marriage, we discovered we were expecting. I had no inclination to sit at home knitting booties. I continued to fly until I could no longer fit into the cockpit, but I did stay on the ground for the delivery! Being pregnant seemed to ignite the flame of competition within me. My friend Dorothy was expecting about the same time. We talked often on the phone, making predictions about who would deliver first. I won. On September 17, 1947, I gave birth to my daughter Marsha and was resting in my room when I heard them wheeling Dorothy down the hall. Perhaps that little victory was the beginning of my racing career.

After Marsha was born, we moved to a little

house in Grabill, several miles northeast of Fort Wayne. When someone wanted a flying lesson, I would get a baby-sitter or take Marsha to my mother's and drive out to Smith Field. I was never gone for more than an hour or two, which to me was no different than other women leaving their children to go to the hairdresser or grocery store. Marsha had no way of knowing that all mommies didn't fly around in the sky.

When I left the WASP, I signed up with the Army Reserve and was commissioned First Lieutenant. Early in 1951 with the Korean conflict heating up, I got a letter saying that if I was available, my service was needed. I sent the application back, explaining that I would like to be based in Fort Wayne because I had a child. I would have gone back in as a captain, and on captain's pay I could have afforded help with the house and child care. I figured they would not let me fly, but I could work in the tower or Operations. Almost immediately I received the following letter from HQ Tenth Air Force:

To 1st Lt. Margaret J. Ringenberg:
1. In accordance with recent directives, the records of female reserve officers and airmen were screened to ascertain whether or not such persons had children under 18 years of age.
2. Your records indicate that you have a child under 18 years of age; therefore, action has been taken to discharge you from the USAF Reserve. You will receive copies of Air Force Reserve Orders indicating such action, under separate cover.
3. In the event that you do not have legal custody of the above mentioned child, notify this headquarters, attn: AFXPRA-3-a, and appropriate action will be taken to revoke the discharge orders.

I doubted that young married men with dependent children got the same consideration. For the second time, my service to my country had been terminated, based solely on my sex. In fact, it wasn't until Jimmy Carter was President that we finally got the recognition we deserved for our military service. During the Gulf War women flew combat missions and no one was more pleased than I was about their achievement. I wondered at the time if they even knew about the WASP. I have since met a few of those young women and know now that they are truly grateful to the women who laid the groundwork for them.

After our second child, Mike, was born in 1953, we moved just a few miles from Grabill to a house on Hosler Road, next door to what later became our permanent home. Bill Witmer, who was a builder, lived next door to us. He was also a pilot and had behind the houses a nice little landing strip that he kept mowed and a J-3 Cub tied to a light pole out back. Instructing had never been easier for me. Some of the builders working nearby would show up on their lunch breaks and take a lesson. We'd go up and fly for a half hour or so while my neighbor watched Mike. It was a great arrangement until another neighbor caused problems. She had a habit of letting her children play behind the house, and they were always leaving their tricycles and ball bats on the landing strip. Bill complained and she procured an attorney to keep me from flying off the strip. My flying made too much noise, she said, and kept her husband from sleeping during the day. It turned out to be a nasty affair before it was done. In the end she had to keep her children off the strip, but I had to stop my backyard flying lessons. Bill could still fly in and out whenever he wanted, but because I had a commercial license, it was not legal for me to fly off an unregistered strip. It was back to Smith Field.

I have been privileged to have some extraordinary experiences, but I have always considered myself an ordinary wife and mother. I think my family would agree. There were times when Marsha was small that I could not get a baby-sitter, so I just took her along. She would sit in the back of the plane and look at books just as other kids did in the back seat of their parents' car. She was fascinated with the sounds that came from the radio. There was a rhythm to the "dits" and "dahs" that she seemed to like. Who knows, maybe those early rhythms planted the seed for her career in music.

Flying just fascinates me. . . It's a challenge. . . and it's the beauty of it. Who has a more changing office than I do?
Margaret Ringenberg

ANOTHER VOICE:

Marsha Wright

(DAUGHTER)

It might seem that my mom was so busy with her flying that she couldn't have had time for me, but that just wasn't true. She was very supportive of my interest in music. From the time I was in second grade until my senior year in high school, she drove me across Fort Wayne every week for piano lessons and later for voice and trumpet lessons too. She was always there for my programs and contests and concerts. We had hundreds of rehearsals at our house and Mom was there, encouraging. If we wanted to sing, she would find a place for us to perform. Now life has come full circle and she is singing in my senior adult choir, Senior Saints, as well as the Praise Choir that I direct.

She was also my Brownie leader when I was in second grade. She continued with us into Girl Scouting and provided others to teach us the things she didn't do, like camping. As most of us liked music, she would help us prepare musical programs to put on in the long-term care unit of a local hospital. All the girls were comfortable with her and I didn't mind having her around, so she was usually our designated driver.

When we got into high school, we could specialize in different areas of scouting. Naturally, we chose to become Wing Scouts. Mom took six of us out to Baer Field to attend Van Stiffler's ground school. We paid our tuition by emptying ash trays and sweeping the floor. Van was a great teacher, but my favorite part of ground school was singing in the hangars during breaks. The acoustics were wonderful! I did pass the written test, which was not an easy task, and three of us went on to earn private licenses. Mom was elated. She endured the antics of a bunch of giggly girls on the ride home and even let us stop at Azar's for a Big Boy and onion rings.

Like all working mothers, I occasionally felt pulled in two directions. One time I had a trip to Wichita to pick up an airplane for the Beechcraft dealer in Fort Wayne. Marsha was in school and Mike was at the baby-sitter's. For some reason, the owner of Beechcraft, Olive Ann Beech, wanted to meet "the lady pilot." We had a quick conversation and I explained that I was in a hurry because I needed to get home in time to pick up my children. I was worried that I might have offended her, but I think she was impressed by the fact that I put my kids first and was not afraid to tell her so. I didn't know it then, but that short conversation probably helped me get an airplane to race a few years later.

When Mike started school, I had cause to question my choice of careers. He was a good boy and we were not aware of any problems until the calls from school began. "Mike is hyperactive," they told us. "Mike is immature." We knew he was able to learn, but he seemed to have so much trouble concentrating. No one seemed to be aware of things like learning disabilities or attention deficit disorders at the time. We worried instead that my flying might be upsetting him or distracting him in some way. We made an appointment for him with a psychiatrist. She found him to be friendly, if a little overactive, but certainly not worried about me. To him, my flying was no more upsetting than if I got in the car and drove to the store. People are injured in auto accidents every day, yet most of us don't think about that every time we get into a car. I have the same approach to flying. It is such a natural thing to me that I never think about anything going wrong. I don't think my children were ever uneasy about it either.

Mike's school years continued to be a struggle, but we tried to keep him involved in other activities. He took drama lessons and enjoyed performing in programs. He was active in Boy Scouts and continues his participation as an adult assistant. Mike lives with us now and is an active member of the church and community. He has a job and is a genuinely caring person, always willing to help anyone in need.

When I first got married, I entertained the idea of teaching Morris to fly, but we could not afford it at the time. Later when money wasn't such an issue, he had no desire to learn. I think some of that hinged on the fact that Mike could not learn to fly. I did get Morris to copilot for me once in awhile. We even won the Kentucky race together two or three times, but for the most part he considered flying to be "my thing." Marsha was the only one who was interested. It was almost as if the desire to fly was passed through the female genes, with the exception of my mother, of course! The next generation seems to be holding true to that theory. Although I have given one of my grandsons flying lessons and two of them have

125

been copilots for me, it seems to be my granddaughter, Jaala, still too young to fly, who is the most interested. Time will tell.

ANOTHER VOICE:

Marsha Wright

When I was in my early teens, Mom would come back from air races with "goody bags" and stories about wonderful sightseeing trips, and parties and travel adventures. We planned that as soon as I was sixteen, the required age, I would go on a race as her copilot. Before that could happen, however, the requirements changed so that copilots had to have a private license. I would just have to learn to fly. Unfortunately, I didn't really like to fly and I did not seem to have a natural aptitude for it. Because Mom had to pay for the use of the plane to teach me, I had to learn in the shortest time possible. The plan was that I would solo on my sixteenth birthday and get my license on my seventeenth so as to generate publicity, which is crucial to getting a sponsor for a race. Along with flying lessons, I was involved in Girl Scouts, band, choir, and church activities as well as a girls' barbershop quartet and a Gospel trio, so it was a busy time for both of us.

I remember the day I soloed at Baer Field. The instructor, my mom, had me taxi out to the middle of the field, where she got out. I was required to take off, fly around the traffic pattern and land. When Mom got out of the plane, there wasn't another plane in sight. She ran up to the control tower so she could talk to me on the radio if I needed help. All of a sudden there were several planes coming in to land, including an airliner that wanted to come straight in. I was having to make a BIG pattern and getting farther and farther from the airport. My mom was aware of a little problem I had; I couldn't find airports from the air very well. Being my mother as well as my instructor, she began to worry that I would get lost, and she asked tower personnel to bring me in. They held up the airliner. Was I impressed!

Mom wanted me to take my flight test from Federal Aviation Authority (FAA) personnel in South Bend rather than Fort Wayne so that there wouldn't be any question about whether I had earned my license. I had to fly the plane up to South Bend in order to complete the required forty hours of flying time before the test. One thing I do enjoy about flying is the scenery. On the way, Mom happened to point out the omni station called Wolf Lake. We joked that it looked like a root beer stand sitting in the middle of a big field. I also commented on the fact that there was no visible lake at Wolf Lake. The test was grueling. The examiner had me run a complete weight and balance on the aircraft even though no one else had ever had to do it. Could they tell just by looking that I disliked math? I couldn't get the numbers to come out right, so the examiner sat down to show me where I was wrong, and I wasn't. The error was in the flight log. When we did start the flight test, he had me turn to the left, turn to the right, turn to the left. If I allowed my altitude to vary more than a hundred feet either way, I would automatically fail the test. At the same time, he kept asking me the reciprocals of compass points. I answered correctly, but it was a struggle. Finally he said, quite smugly I thought, "Where are we? You must always know where you are." My heart nearly stopped. I had been concentrating on his questions so much that I had failed to look at the map in my lap or even out the window. I didn't have the foggiest notion where we were. Desperate, I looked down and there was the "root beer stand." I pointed to Wolf Lake on the map, turned to him and in my sweetest voice said, "We're right here." I wish I could have captured his expression on film.

"Take me back to the airport," he muttered. I passed.

Marsha soloed on her sixteenth birthday and earned her private license on her seventeenth as planned, but she actually learned to fly by rote. She passed her flight test because she did what I told her. She knew all the right answers when the examiner asked her. I wonder if she might like to really learn to fly some day, but I know that it's music, not flying, that is her passion. She did beat me once in the Indiana F.A.I.R. race. I sent one of my students with her as copilot because it was his plane. I often chose newly licensed pilots to fly with her, feeling that they did not take flying for granted and were more cautious and willing to follow a map. She was so proud of the trophy that she had it put in the trophy case at Fort Wayne Bible College, where she was a student. A few days later, the race committee notified me that there had been a mistake in scoring and everyone had been knocked down a notch. They wanted Marsha to return the trophy. "How much do the trophies cost?" I asked. "I'll send you the money to buy another one. I'm not going to ask her to take hers out of the trophy case." So she didn't win the race, but she still beat me and I think that was enough for her.

ANOTHER VOICE:

Marsha Wright

My mother has always insisted on doing her best in everything. No halfway jobs for her. She expected the same from me. I especially remember one time at Homecoming in high school. Our band was going to march down the street to the elementary school, and the director had come up with the idea of a creative hat contest. He wanted each of us to design a crazy hat to wear in the parade. Most kids just put pins on a baseball cap or a purple ribbon on a straw hat. But would my mother settle for that? Not on your life. We got an octagonal box, covered it with foil and stuck white chicken feathers and other things on it. It was utterly outlandish, but I won first prize and Mom was content.

When I was sixteen, I was to sing the solo to the popular Singing Nun's song, "Dominique." It was in French and I didn't know how to pronounce the words. Mom came to the rescue with one of her students who was French Canadian. Later when I was invited to sing in a production at Franke Park Festival Music Theater, I was so timid I balked at going to the first rehearsal. I didn't know anyone, and the people were quite different from those in my church. Mom's hand was on my back the whole time, pushing, pushing. I was enjoying myself until I heard that we would have to do a costume change between scenes, and men and women would be sharing the changing area. I should have known better than to panic. Mom had a solution. She had Aunt Vi make me a camisole that I could wear under both outfits. She always had an answer. I think she liked the challenge.

Mom also pushed me into swimming lessons and eventually into getting my lifesaving certificate. There came a time when she finally pushed too hard. She had driven several of us girls to the YMCA in Auburn for a lesson. When I hesitated, she insisted that I was perfectly capable of doing my little "doggie paddle" across the deep end of the pool. Apparently the instructor didn't share Mom's confidence because she jumped in the water fully clothed to rescue me. I think Mom felt bad about that one. Sometimes I catch myself pushing my own children to do things "just a little better." I know where I learned that.

Steve Wright
(SON-IN-LAW)

When I was in second grade, my father was a pastor in Auburn, Indiana. Whenever we had occasion to go into Fort Wayne by way of Amstutz Road, my dad would point out the house with the grass strip and the airplane out back. That was where Margaret Ringenberg lived. Years later, as Alumni Coordinator for Fort Wayne Bible College, my dad sometimes traveled with The Ambassadors, a student quintet that represented the college. When he came home he would tell me about the members of the group, especially a girl named Marsha Ringenberg. Later I became a student at the college and my dad introduced me to her. Eventually we started dating and it came time for me to meet her parents.

When I first met Margaret, I was a little intimidated. After all, she had invested so much in Marsha. She had encouraged her in swimming, scouting, band, choir, piano, and of course, flying. Marsha participated in church activities, Festival Music Theater, and Girl Scout Roundup. I asked myself why I thought I was good enough for her. I didn't even know what I was going to do for a living. Margaret was wise enough to be friendly and gracious to me. If she had any negative feelings about me, she kept them to herself. When we did marry, Margaret and Morris were very supportive, but never intrusive even though we lived in the same community. After the grandchildren started to arrive, we discovered there was one reason Margaret would pass up a flying trip — a chance to hold a grandchild. I saw a tender side of her I had not seen before.

There have been many times that she has spared no time or expense to help us in whatever way she could. When Marsha and our son Joe suffered from migraines, Margaret not only helped out around the house, but sought solutions to the problem. She loves problem solving and can no more let one go than a dog can let go of a bone. One time, Marv Berger was working a street fair and needed sixty pounds of confectioner's sugar and a nacho cheese warmer from Cincinnati.

Margaret and Marv, who is also a pilot, often helped each other out, so she volunteered to pick them up. She came by the house Saturday morning to see if anyone wanted to ride with her. We were expecting company at 5:30 and I hated to leave Marsha with all the preparations, but this was a chance to go flying! "Can you have him back by four?" Marsha asked.

Margaret looked at her watch, did some mental figuring and said, "No, but I can have him back by five." Marsha agreed to that and we were off. It was a beautiful, cloudless day and she let me fly most of the way. We landed at Sunken Lunken on the Ohio River, taxied up to air service and went in to pick up the cargo. We flew back to Baer Field, dropped off the freight, and took the plane back to Smith Field. Then we rushed home for the evening's activities. I was home by 5:02. She is a woman of her word.

✈

Let Me Tell You About the Time. . .

Many times instructing is as simple as meeting a student at the airport, flying around for half an hour and going home. But, there are times when it becomes a learning experience for me as well. On one such occasion, my student, Dan Nolan, came to me and explained that his friend, Ken Kirts, needed to get to South Carolina for the Darlington Auto Race, where he had been the announcer for many years. Ken, who was a writer, also wanted to do a story on a church in West Virginia where the people handled poisonous snakes as part of their faith. Dan wanted to fly him and make a stop in Cleveland for the National Air Race, but he needed an instructor along. How could I resist such an offer?

133

A few days later, I was telling Keith Stevenson about the trip. "You're a lucky one," he said. Keith had an instrument ticket, I remembered, and although I had a military instrument ticket, I was not instrument rated at the time. I asked him to join us. With four people and lots of camera equipment, the Cherokee 180, a four place (seat) airplane, was packed tightly when we left Fort Wayne the following Saturday for Cleveland. Edna Gardner Whyte, a pioneer in women's aviation, was pylon racing, and she asked me to time her for some test runs. Watching the race was exciting, but as I saw the airplanes nearly touching the ground as they took the turns, I decided that pylon racing was not for me.

As soon as the field opened up after the race, we were on our way to West Virginia. Having heard of snake-handling sects who believe that their faith will protect them from poisonous viper bites, I was intrigued at the idea of seeing it firsthand. When we arrived at the airport there was a car waiting to take us to the hotel. I thought I should clean up a little, and we agreed to meet in the lobby a few minutes later to go to dinner. I changed into heels, a clean skirt and blouse, and dabbed on a touch of make-up. It was already 7:30 and I told the guys I thought we should be getting to the church. "There's no hurry," Ken said. "They don't get worked up until ten or eleven o'clock." I was afraid to ask if he meant the people or the snakes. He studied my appearance. "You're too dressed up," he said. "Maybe you should change back into your traveling clothes and wash off the make-up. You'll fit in better that way." We had dinner and then headed for the hills, and I do mean HILLS. It was way back there! When we finally got to the church and parked the car, we had to cross over a creek on a footbridge and climb a small hill. Nolan kept repeating, "I'm not using any bright lights to take pictures of poisonous snakes." I sensed his reluctance to even be in the same room with snakes, poisonous or not.

He didn't have to worry. Just as we reached the church, we met a couple coming out. "One of the local men got drunk and came up here and dragged his wife out by the hair," they told us. "The noise upset the snakes and they had to remove them from the church." So much for Ken's story. We did stay and watch the service for a little while, or rather, I watched the people, most of them poor and many without teeth. It was not at all like my congregation at home. When we realized the service could go on for hours, we slipped out and went back to the hotel.

The next day we flew to the Darlington Auto Race. Keith and I checked the weather and watched the race. It was fun listening to Ken announce the race and watching Nolan snap pictures, but the noise was deafening. The trip home was uneventful. Ken didn't get his story and we didn't get to see the snakes, but it was an eye-opening experience for all of us. Nolan was happy, though. He got to fly the plane.

By the winter of 1976, I had been employed at Fort Wayne airports as an instructor for many years, and even though I had the manager's approval, I started to feel guilty about taking time away from my students to fly the Powder Puff Derby, in which, by then, I had been participating every year since 1957. Then one icy day in February, I slipped on the ramp at the airport and broke my ankle. While I was laid up in the hospital, I began to worry. What if I couldn't race this year? I tried to be optimistic, so I sent for some race kits and entered one I hadn't flown before. A few weeks later, the manager of Consolidated Airways came to see me at home. "Would you consider coming back to work on a limited basis?" he asked. "I know you can't fly, but you could just come to the office and talk to the students." I was on crutches, unable to do simple housework, and I would lose my small workman's compensation, but I agreed. I enjoyed being back at the airport until the day the manager noticed that I had marked off the dates for the Angel Derby Race. He became agitated, telling me that if I could race, I could instruct. He seemed to forget that he wasn't paying me to come into the office. I was a flight instructor; I didn't get paid unless I was in an airplane with the prop turning.

There was more trouble ahead. When I asked one day for a Friday afternoon and Saturday off to fly the Fair Ladies Annual Indiana Race (F.A.I.R.), the manager told me, "You're going to have to make a choice. Instructing or racing." I was shocked; I couldn't believe this was happening. I was a good flight instructor and I loved my students, but I also loved to race. Why couldn't I do both?

Morris knew how upset I was. "Just tell them at the airport to get another instructor," he advised. Consequently, I went back to the airport and walked into the manager's office to tell him to get someone to replace me, but he was on the phone. Close to tears, I fled to the restroom where he couldn't see me cry. When I went back to the office, his secretary said he had gone to Muncie. I got my things and left. Driving home, my spirits sank as I thought about the students and the nice airplanes I was giving up.

Then a funny thing happened. My students began to call. I tried to assure them that there were plenty of other good instructors at the airport, but before long a few of them joined a flying club and convinced me to continue their lessons as a freelance instructor. More good things happened. Mr. James Kelly, who owned a Lance and a Navajo, offered me some work. Mrs. Kelly liked to visit her sister in Atlanta, and the Kellys were building several nursing homes in Indiana, Ohio, and Washington D.C. They needed a pilot. When they decided to look for property on which to build a home, they had me fly them over the area until they found the ideal location near Cedar Creek in northeast Allen County, Indiana. Then I got several trips to Williamsburg, Virginia, as the Kellys went to look at houses they could show their architect. There is an old saying: "When God closes a door, he always opens a window." And when God opened the window, I did what I do best. I flew through it.

I enjoy instructing very much. Each time I take a student out, I can see an improvement. I have a captive audience. I get 'em up there and they don't have any choice but to learn! —Margaret Ringenberg

ANOTHER VOICE:

Bruce Bone
(FORMER STUDENT)

My brother had been a Navy pilot during World War II so I had always wanted to learn to fly in the worst way. I chose Margaret as an instructor because my wife was going to take lessons too and I thought she might be more comfortable with a woman instructor. On our first ride with Margaret, we flew up to Michigan, landed and had lunch and then started back to Fort Wayne. Somewhere between Waterloo and Auburn the motor started to sputter. Before long it became clear to me that we were going down. Margaret took over the controls and nursed the airplane into the Auburn airport. Almost as soon as we touched down, the motor stopped and the airplane had to be towed away. I was terrorized, of course, but Margaret acted as if it was no more of a problem to her than doing housework. It would have been easy to quit right then, but Margaret's professionalism gave me the confidence to continue.

I was very aggressive about finishing up the forty hours I needed to get my private license. I probably gave Margaret fits wanting to fly four or five times a week even though she had a lot of other students at the time too. Since I owned my own business the only time I could fly was early in the morning or late afternoon. One morning in December 1976 when Margaret came zipping into the airport about 7:00 a.m. to give me one more ride before sending me to the examiner, she slipped on the ice near the terminal and broke her ankle. We rushed her to Parkview Hospital where she had a cast put on.

Like I said, I was aggressive about finishing my instruction so in spite of the fact that she was laid up in a hospital bed, I showed up with my log book for her to sign. She made quite a picture, lying in bed with her leg in traction, talking to the flight examiner on the phone. Nothing was impossible for her. In her quiet, cordial manner she would overcome every hurdle put in front of her.

Most of my instruction with Margaret had been at Baer Field in Fort Wayne where there was a hard surface runway. Sometime after getting my license I bought a plane with six places. My wife, Suzanne, my son and I took a trip up to Lake Wawasee about thirty or forty miles northwest of Fort Wayne. The landing strip was short, only about 1,000 feet, and covered with grass about a foot high. I came in for a nice smooth landing, applied the brakes, and nothing happened! I began to slide on the wet grass. At the end of the runway was a barbed wire fence, and beyond that, a road, so I knew I had to do something quickly. I put it into a side slide and finally came to a stop just short of the fence. When I got out of the plane, I was shaking badly. It didn't help matters when the airport manager walked up and said, "That was the worst landing I've ever seen." I immediately called Margaret.

"You meet me at the airport at 8 o'clock tomorrow morning," she said. The next day we flew back to that grassy airstrip and landed. Then we took off and landed again and again, at least ten or twelve times until I could do it right. I went on to get my instrument ticket and commercial license as well as log between eight and ten thousand hours of flying time, but I owe it all to those early lessons with Margaret. No matter what comes my way, I know I have been well equipped.

Steve Wright

I remember an incident at Baer Field that brought home to me once again what a remarkable person Margaret is. She once slipped in water dripping from an air-conditioner at the airport and fell and cracked her head. She was conscious, but unable to speak or move. Her blood spread into the puddle of water and made it appear that she was lying in a pool of blood. When a secretary came out and saw her, she rushed back inside to call for help, explaining only that there had been "an accident at Baer Field." Imagine Margaret's surprise when several fire departments appeared on the scene. As soon as they realized the nature of the "accident," they called for an ambulance. When the paramedics arrived to transport her to Lutheran Hospital, however, Margaret refused to lie down on the gurney. She insisted on sitting up all the way to the hospital, where they stitched her head and checked for other injuries. When they finished, she went back to the airport and flew for an hour with a student before she finally went home with a terrific headache. When I later told the story to the men with whom I was working, pouring concrete, one crusty old cigar-smoking guy said, "That's one damn tough mother-in-law." We still get laughs from that one.

The year 1976 marked fifty years since the Post Office turned transportation of the Air Mail over to private contractors. It was to be commemorated by having volunteer members of the Silver Wings Fraternity fly the route from New York to San Francisco and from San Francisco to New York over the original route. Josephine Richardson and I, both members of Silver Wings, were to fly the leg from Chicago to Bryan, Ohio, using my Mooney. The Mooney had not been flown for awhile because I had taken it in to have the engine rebuilt just before I broke my ankle. Marv Berger, a friend from Fort Wayne, had to fly it back for me because I was unable to use the brake. Then it sat idle for several months. As the Illinois race was coming up, I wanted to see how the new engine would perform before the race.

Josephine came to Fort Wayne and together we headed for Chicago. I used the throttle setting I would use in the race to see how the airplane would do on gas. When we arrived at Chicago Midway, I told them to refuel the airplane. I was incredulous when they told me it took twenty-four gallons. That was impossible. The trip had taken less than an hour, and ten to twelve gallons would be normal. I thought they were trying to take advantage of me, but there was no time to get into it because the press was covering the event. When we got back into the plane, it wouldn't start. I tried until I ran the battery down and then asked for a "jump," but still it wouldn't start. Finally, I ran over to one of the operators at the airport and borrowed an airplane. We flew it to Bryan, Ohio, and delivered the mail, but we were three hours late. We had missed the luncheon planned to commemorate the event and most of the press coverage. After a few pictures, we flew back to Fort Wayne to drop Josephine off, then I flew back to Chicago to return the borrowed plane.

Meanwhile, the shop had taken the Mooney in and gone over it. The mechanics discovered that when the engine had been rebuilt, a bolt had been run up through the carburetor. The airplane really had taken twenty-four gallons of gasoline because fuel had been running out underneath. The mechanic contacted the people who had rebuilt the engine. "You'd better send someone down here right away," he told them over the phone. "The press was here when it happened and, if Margaret wants to give you some bad publicity, she has it all in black and white." I didn't stay around. I found a pilot I knew and caught a flight back to Fort Wayne on a mail plane loaded with freight. When I went back to get the plane, I immediately took it to my own mechanic, Bob Harrold, and had him go over it with me. Before a race, I like to go over the plane for safety reasons. If it's a plane with retractable gear, I like to make sure the gear is up there tight. I like to confirm that my spark plugs are in excellent condition and that all the harnesses in the plane are in good shape. I want to know if the doors seal tight. Bob not only takes care of the airplane I race, but several others that I fly. I know that I can call him from any place and describe my problems. He will tell me the truth if he thinks I should not fly it. We all need someone we can trust, but when it comes to airplanes it's essential.

"Never leave the ground with the motor leaking."—Early air mail regulation

ANOTHER VOICE:

Rev. G. Michael Livingston
(STUDENT AND CLOSE PERSONAL FRIEND)

I was the pastor of the Grabill (Indiana) Missionary Church when Margaret who was a member of the congregation offered to teach me to fly. At the time, I didn't give it much thought, although as a boy I had dreamed of becoming a pilot. Some months later, however, while a passenger on a commercial airliner, I happened to read an article about the risk of burnout among pastors. I admitted with concern that I fell into the high risk category as one who had no interests or hobbies outside my church. Pondering my options, I immediately eliminated woodworking and gardening, having neither the talent nor inclination for either. Then Margaret's offer came to mind. She could teach me to fly! Could that, I wondered, be my outlet?

On the seventh of February 1980, Margaret gave me my first lesson in a Piper Cherokee 160 PA-32. It was the first of many hours we would spend flying together even beyond the time necessary for me to acquire both a VFR license and instrument rating. In all of the United States there could not have been a better flight instructor for me. She gave me confidence, and whenever I thought I couldn't do something, she would just keep encouraging and prodding until I did it.

It seemed to me that everyone at the Fort Wayne airports knew her. At times we would taxi out for a lesson, and Margaret would radio tower personnel with our call letters. Picking up the microphone, she would say, "This is 38-Whiskey." Immediately, tower personnel would call her by name, and everyone would be assured that things were under control and there was no need to worry about the inexperienced student pilot at the controls.

The first time I was to solo, a frightening prospect without her comforting presence beside me, she asked for and received permission from tower personnel to stand out on the edge of the runway while I did a "go-around" and a touchdown." I have often wondered if they ever allowed anyone else to do that.

Even though I have lived in California now for eight years, I still travel back to Indiana to take my biennial flight tests with Margaret, not only because I feel more comfortable with her, but because I know she will not pass me unless she feels I am capable of flying the airplane. Who will give me my biennials if she retires? Will I ever trust anyone else as much as I trust her? I guess she will just have to keep flying forever because, frankly, I can't picture myself in an airplane without the knowledge that Margaret will be there if I need her.

ANOTHER VOICE:

Tony Niewyk
(ATTORNEY, PARTNER IN BAKER AND DANIELS, A FIRM FOR WHICH MARGARET HAS FLOWN)

Margaret often flew for my firm. She just loved to fly our Bonanza. One thing that has always amazed me about her is her uncanny sense of hearing. She has flown a Cherokee P-28 for years without a headset. She is always tuned in, always listening. If there is any little change in the sound of the engine, she hears it immediately and instinctively knows what to do. As an instrument pilot, she flies many different kinds of airplanes, but she is so in tune with the airplane, nothing seems to rattle her.

Flying with her, I would sometimes wonder what I would do if something happened to her and I had to fly the plane. I decided to learn. When I started taking lessons with Margaret, it occurred to me that every time she took a student up, she was taking her life in her hands. At any time, a student could make a mistake and put the airplane in danger. Margaret never seemed to worry about that. She was very patient and always sensitive to my state of mind. In my profession, I have to have the ability to conceal my feelings, but Margaret was always able to read the signals and know if I was "uptight." She taught me to be aware of my own emotional state—not to fly when I was too tired or when I had something on my mind that would impair my judgment.

I'll never forget the day I soloed for the first time. She knew better than I when I was ready. I don't know how many hours I had been flying, but it was more than the minimum required. That day, we were sitting on the ground with the engine running. She opened the door and got out. "You can do this," she said. I wasn't so sure, but her confidence gave me confidence. I did it and that date has always stuck in my mind—7/7/87. Later I went on to get my private license, and eventually my instrument ticket.

ANOTHER VOICE:

Marvin Berger
(FELLOW PILOT, AND FRIEND)

In 1966 I bought a Mooney airplane which at that time was considered a high performance aircraft. I planned to use it in our expanding business, but with the airplane came the need for me to obtain an IFR rating. Many friends recommended Margaret Ringenberg to me for IFR instruction. Having a lady instructor wasn't the most popular approach at that time, and I thought the suggestion was a little "far out." When I met her in the coffee shop at Smith Field, I made an unusual request. I wanted to fly every day, regardless of the weather, so that I could get experience in all types of conditions. Margaret agreed and because of our arrangement, she was able to prepare me for my check ride in a minimum amount of time.

Those days were just the beginning of a life-long friendship with many trips and flying experiences along the way. One such experience that occurred during my IFR flight training sticks in my mind. While performing time turns to the left, we discovered that the turns were not consistent and whenever we turned there was a loud bang in the fuselage. It was quite unnerving when it was later diagnosed as a broken engine mount.

One time we planned to take our employees to Florida for a little winter break. We had enough passengers to warrant taking two airplanes. Margaret had to stop in Indianapolis to pick up two of her passengers. It was a very windy day, to say the least, and no one had landed at Eagle Creek Airport on that day until Margaret made her landing! After she had shut the engine down and unloaded, the line boys proceeded to congratulate Margaret's husband for a great landing. (He doesn't fly!)

After several years of owning the Mooney, we advanced to a twin-engine Baron. Knowing that Margaret was always available to help area pilots, I called on her for multi-engine training. Around 1967, my cousin graduated from the Air Force Academy. He wanted to get his private license during the three weeks before his next assignment, which would require him to log forty hours of flight training and pass the written exam. With Margaret as his instructor, he not only completed the training, logged the necessary hours, and passed his flight test, he did it all in ten days!

Once an instructor, always an instructor I've found. Even after the lessons end, Margaret can't stop instructing. While it may bother some pilots, I have always felt that it is just the dedication of a good teacher. Without a doubt, Margaret has contributed more to general aviation in our community than any other person I know. She has a unique approach to instructing. She will let you do your thing and then ask a pointed question. "What are you doing?" or "Where are you going?" It certainly gets your attention. Her teaching may have saved my life and that of a friend when in 1997 we survived a crash landing. Even the FAA could not believe that we landed the plane in a hay field in the mountains of Pennsylvania and walked away with minor injuries. Whether it was Margaret's instruction, my own ability, or a combination of both, I'll never know. At any rate I thank Margaret for her dedication and devotion to the art of flying.

PART FOUR

Flying For The Fun Of It

"Flying, someone wisely said, is ten percent technique and ninety percent head work. This goes for a flight around the airport, over the ocean, or across the United States. . . The contestant must know her airplane. At what altitude it is fastest, how much fuel does it burn, is it better to fly it at a slower, more economical fuel consumption and stop less, or is it better to 'pour on the coal,' go fast, but stop an extra time or two? All these things must be in her book of knowledge."-
Official program of All Woman Transcontinental Air Race, 1957

✈

Racing 101

When I say I race airplanes, most people immediately think of a speed race, but there are several kinds of racing in which speed is not necessarily a factor. In an efficiency race, for example, the pilot tries to get the most miles per hour on the least amount of gas. It involves starving the engine, which is not good for the airplane. I never liked to fly efficiency races and, in fact, I don't think there are any anymore.

A proficiency race is a little more complicated. Before the race, and even before knowing the exact course, the pilots must declare in writing how much fuel they will use and what speed they will average. The winner is seldom more than a tenth of a gallon off in fuel or more than a few seconds in time. The Illi-Nines, the Illinois branch of the Ninety-Nines, an international women pilots' organization, have a race every year. Featuring both speed and proficiency categories, it is a relatively short race, about two hundred miles, around Illinois. I have flown every one of them, some 21 in all. The Illinois race usually comes just before the Air Race Classic, so I like to fly it as a warm-up for the long race. Pylon racing, a kind of speed racing, is something I have never done. Racers fly so low, the planes almost touch the ground. At the risk of repeating myself, that's not for me. I'm not a daredevil.

The transcontinental race in which I have competed every year was first called the Powder Puff and then the Air Race Classic (ARC). It is an all women's race. Only once in 1975, did a man try to enter the race and he was refused. He sued and lost. A U.S. District Court judge refused to order the race organizers to admit a male entry, saying that the Constitution did not guarantee his right to enter. The ARC remains an all-female race, since to enter, one must be a member of the Ninety-Nines, which is a woman pilot's organization. Thus, in the ARC, both pilot and copilot must be female and both must be licensed, although at one time, the copilot was not required to be. There is no upper age limit. Indeed, I know women who wait for their Social Security checks to come in so they can go racing. One of the pilots must have an instrument ticket, though, and at least a hundred hours of cross-country experience. Any number of planes can be entered. Powder Puff entries reached about two hundred planes at one time, but now it is much more expensive to fly, and manufacturers are not producing as many planes. Forty or fifty contestants is more realistic now. It isn't uncommon for women to fly rented planes, which are better in some ways, because they are well taken care of and are inspected every hundred hours.

The race starts and ends in a different location each year and is not necessarily coast to coast, although it is always around two thousand miles in length, with a number of stops along the way. While the pilot is on the ground at a designated stop, the clock stops. Contestants have up to four days to complete the course. Although the impulse is to land and get going as quickly as possible, I have learned that sometimes sitting tight and waiting for the wind to change or bad weather to move out can make a big difference in one's score. Sometimes in an emergency, or if she needs fuel, a pilot is forced to land at an unauthorized field. In that case, the time keeps going which cuts into her score. Because of the many factors involved, the first to finish is not necessarily the winner. This is the twist on a speed race.

I began flying the Powder Puff Derby in 1957 and flew the last twenty of them. I have flown its successor, the Air Race Classic, every year since. I never won the Powder Puff and I have won the Classic only once — so far — but I am proud to say that I have never begun a race I didn't finish. After so many years, of course, I have a great many friends on the racing circuit. I'll admit that socializing is an important part of the race for me too.

✈

Why Aren't You Flying?

When the All Woman Transcontinental Air Race (AWTAR), nicknamed the Powder Puff Derby, came through Fort Wayne in 1956, it opened up a whole new aspect of flying to me. Members of the Indiana Chapter of the Ninety-Nines were the hostesses, providing snacks, rides, and other help to the racers. My job was to direct the airplanes in. Because Baer Field was a "must" stop that year, everyone came in. There was to be a bonus of eight hundred dollars for the first pilot to land. I was excited just to be a part of it. More than once that day, people along the fence would call out, "Margaret, why aren't you flying the race?" I laughed. Racing is costly; I had two small children and we were in the process of buying a house. It was out of the question. Or was it? After the race, I couldn't put it out of my mind. On Sundays or holidays whenever I happened to be at the airport, I started looking at the airplanes from a different perspective.

Then one day, when I walked into the hangar, I spotted a Cessna 172 with "Crosby Boat Company" scrawled across the side. This was a Grabill company and I just happened to know the president. I stopped in his office for a little chat the next day. "I want to fly the next Powder Puff," I announced, explaining that the race would be from California to Philadelphia and then adding that I wanted to represent Crosby. By the time I finished my pitch, he had offered the plane. Now I needed a sponsor. Sam Fletcher suggested that he and several other friends put in $50 each. No one wanted his name on the plane, so they suggested I use some good non-profit organization. Being a Girl Scout leader, it occurred to me that it would be good publicity for the local council. When I checked with the Girl Scout office, they thought it was a great idea, as long as it wouldn't cost them anything. Their phones started ringing as soon as it came out in the paper. People thought the profit from Girl Scout cookie sales was being used to sponsor an air race! I have since learned that getting a sponsor isn't always the expedient thing to do. If I don't win, there is nothing in it for the sponsor, and it puts undue pressure on me.

I sent in the twenty-five dollar entry fee, hoping it would get there before the deadline. The day my confirmation came I ran around shouting to anyone who would listen, "I made it! I'm number 24!" Mine was the only entry from northern

Indiana. I asked my sister-in-law, Lois Laymon, to be my copilot. While she was not a licensed pilot, she did know how to work a radio and she would be a great morale booster. We began discussing how we could keep our expenses to a minimum. Our plan was to eat as little as possible, a hamburger at lunch, maybe, and a bowl of soup for supper. If necessary, we would sleep in the airplane, although the cabin of the 172, about as wide as two chairs, would not provide the most comfortable sleeping arrangements, especially since the seats did not even tip back. We didn't care. We were going to be in a race and that was all that mattered.

Then, just a few days before we were to leave for the start of the race in San Carlos, California, my mother-in-law, who was suffering with cancer, took a turn for the worse. When she slipped into a coma, Lois came to me. "I think I should stay in case she comes out of the coma," she said. "but I want you to go on."

"No," I protested. "There will be other races. I don't have to fly this one." Morris and the rest of the family insisted. So much preparation had gone into the race, they argued. It would be a shame not to go. They all wanted me to go, but who could I get to copilot at such short notice? I thought of my friend, Marty Wyall, who was also a former WASP. She had five children, the youngest of whom was only an infant, but she jumped at the chance. Her poor husband was in shock, I think. At least Morris had been given time to get used to the idea. We scrambled to do last-minute preparations. Pilots and copilots always wore matching outfits so luckily Marty was able to fit into Lois's dress, but she needed to hurry out to buy a pair of black shoes. Then we were on our way.

Fort Wayne's Baer Field was not a "must" stop on the race to Philadelphia, but I planned a quick stop there to meet Morris and the kids. Since it was early afternoon, we thought we could just refuel, visit with our families for a few minutes and keep going. Rules did not permit night flying; consequently, pilots coming in later would have to spend the night. First I had to deal with the guys at the airport who were quite upset that we had flown nonstop from Nebraska. "There can't be any fuel in the carburetor," one of the mechanics complained as he got up to look in the tanks. But there was. We had picked up a tailwind and come in with gas to spare. I might have been a novice at racing, but I knew my airplane.

I scanned the crowd, looking for Morris and the kids. They weren't there. As I walked around the airplane, someone at the fence said, "So sorry to hear, Margaret." I rushed over to the fence.

"Why? What happened?" I asked, fearing the worst.

"I thought you knew. Morris' mother passed away." My family had all gone to Cleveland for the funeral. I realized that Morris had kept the news from me so I would continue the race, but finishing was the last thing on my mind at that point. I got a ride home and tried to call Morris in Cleveland. He had started home. "There's nothing you can do," he told me when he arrived. "You should go on. Everyone in the family wants you to finish." We talked late into the night.

We went on to finish the race, but the joy had gone out of it. The end of the race brought more bad news. I was called before the judges. My score would have put me in thirteenth place, not bad for a first try, but, they informed me, I had been disqualified.

"But why?" I cried. I wasn't prepared for the answer. Way back at our first stop in Elko, Nevada, someone had reported that my propeller was still going when Marty punched the time clock and raced to the plane, a clear violation of the rules. The engine must be off and the propeller completely stopped before the copilot can get out of the plane. I couldn't understand. Going over it in my mind, I was sure the engine was off. Marty and I were wearing full, almost circular, skirts and I was sure that if the propeller had been turning, her skirt would have flown way up. I didn't remember that happening. It didn't matter.

"We had a report from Elko," the judges said. "We're sorry, but those are the rules. You're disqualified." I learned from that first race that there was more to flying races than just flying. There are all the other details that come into the picture, but I have discovered over the years that the problems are all part of the learning process. The race of 1957 wasn't a total loss, however. Each of us won a transistor radio! Moreover, the winner of the event was a former WASP, so at least we had kept it among friends.

Marty Wyall
(COPILOT AND FRIEND)

My family will never let me forget the story of how I became Margaret's first copilot in the 1957 Powder Puff Derby. The morning Margaret stopped at the house, things were already hectic. My two-year-old, Peter, had just poured lotion on the piano keys and I was busy trying to clean it up as well as tend to my seven-week-old daughter and three school-age boys, who were also at home. I assumed that she was going to ask me to baby-sit Mike and Marsha, since I was more or less homebound anyway. Instead, she asked, "Marty, how would you like to go to California?"

"I'd love to," I answered without hesitation. "Just tell me when." She explained that she was going to be a contestant in the All Woman Transcontinental Air Race. She needed a copilot, since her sister-in-law, Lois, would not be able to go because her mother was very ill. The more she talked, the more excited I got. "When are you leaving?"

"Tomorrow."

"Tomorrow!" I exclaimed. It looked impossible. How could I make all the arrangements in twenty-four hours? Margaret explained that the main reason she wanted to go on this race was because Fort Wayne was going to be one of the stops. If I couldn't go, she said, she would have to withdraw from the race. "Margaret," I said. "If I can get my mother to come up from Indianapolis to baby-sit, I can take care of the other problems." I called my mother, and she said she would be on the afternoon bus. The next problem was a little more difficult. Since I was still nursing my infant daughter, I had to go to my doctor to get a formula for her and pills to dry up my milk. I didn't realize how uncomfortable I would be for a few days because of that decision. My mother arrived and as we worked out a schedule for the next two weeks, I realized how lucky I was that she was willing to take on such a big job at age sixty-two. But all the details seemed to be falling into place. Even Lois's race outfit fit me perfectly.

I was a little more concerned about what my husband, Gene, would say. I decided not to call him at work, but wait to break the news until he came home for dinner. He was happy to see my mother. She was a teetotaler and a minister's wife so he liked to tease her about getting into his liquor. His mood changed, however, when he found out that I was planning to "desert my family." It was not a happy dinner hour. "You can just stop at Reno on your way and get a divorce!" he shouted. "You're going to make it difficult on everyone else just so you can go flying across the country!" He told me I couldn't go.

But I had already made up my mind. Promptly at nine o'clock the next morning we took off westbound from Smith Field in a Cessna 172. We had lovely weather, and spent the first night in Cheyenne, Wyoming. I was amazed at how much aviation had changed since I had stopped flying in 1948. Omnidirectional aids had spread across the country and instruments were installed in the planes to give visual readings of our position rather than the low frequency radio aids we had used in the 1940's. Another interesting aspect of flying across the country was seeing the progress of the Interstate Highway System which President Eisenhower had initiated. I was especially interested, since Gene was very much involved in the construction of Interstate 69 back in Indiana. We stopped at the race stops on the way to California in order to get a feel for the layout of each airport. We spent the weekend in Fresno visiting Ringenberg relatives and then went on to San Carlos, where the airplane was impounded and inspected.

When the race started, we took off in the order of our race number, which was 24. The race route was almost a straight line from San Carlos to Philadelphia, Pennsylvania. When we landed at Baer Field in Fort Wayne, the local television cameras were there, plus a reporter from the Journal Gazette. My dad even drove up from Indianapolis to join in the excitement. Although Gene was still angry, I think even he was excited and interested in the events of the last week. The next morning we flew on to Philadelphia, the terminus of the race. We were happy to have completed the course and eager to see how we had fared in the standings. It was a great disappointment when we found that we had been disqualified, but it was a lesson well learned. What we had been accused of was not a serious infraction or a question of safe operation of the airplane, but it taught us to be more alert to the details of the procedure of clocking in and out.

In the 1950s the AWTAR was a wonderful opportunity to test one's flying abilities. The committee members were competent pilots themselves, and the race was run entirely by women, many of whom were former WASPs and friends of ours. I enjoyed myself so much that in 1958 I entered the race as pilot of a Cessna 182. I had eleven sponsors, mostly Gene's construction friends, much to his dismay.

✈

Get to the Finish Line First

There were sixty-nine entries in the 1958 Powder Puff Derby, but there was only one I needed to beat — Sarah Stronk of Charleston, South Carolina. I didn't know Sarah, so I certainly didn't have any personal vendetta against her. It was just that George Bailey, who owned the Beechcraft Bonanza I wanted to fly, had put one condition on the race. "Get to the finish line first." It seems that would be the whole point of racing, but in the case of the Powder Puff and now the Air Race Classic, it isn't. The transcontinental is a handicapped race. A par speed is established for each airplane, based on the manufacturer's performance figures, flight tests and other data. In other words the airplane is assigned a speed rating which is the normal speed that it can be expected to make. If a contestant averages better than that speed, she gains points. If she averages less, she loses points. The person with the most points wins, and this cannot be determined until everyone has finished the race. Thus, crossing the finish line first did not mean that I would win the race. More than likely, I would not. But George knew, and so did I, that the first one across the finish line would get the lion's share of the publicity. We did not know at the time that the Beech dealer in Charleston, the terminus of the race, had given his pilot, Sarah, the same directive. What made it interesting was that we had identical planes right down to the colors — yellow and white.

I was the first to have my papers in order at the start and the first to have my plane inspected. When I left San Diego with my sister-in-law Lois as copilot, I was determined to get to Charleston first; but when we landed in Tyler, Texas, for an overnight stop, we found Sarah's plane already parked in the first spot. She had not been there long enough to get out of the airport yet, so several of us shared a ride to the hotel. We even had dinner together. "What time are you going out in the morning?" I asked innocently between bites. "Maybe we can share a ride."

"We don't know yet," Sarah answered. "We want to check the weather first."

We said goodnight and when we got to our room, I told Lois I was going to call the front desk and leave a wake-up call. When I told the operator that we wanted a three o'clock wake-up, she said, "Oh, the other girls are getting up at three also." So that was their game!

When three o'clock came it didn't take us long to get ready. We didn't carry a suitcase so all we had to do was put the same dresses back on and we were out the door. Rushing down the hall, we got to the elevator just in time to see the accordion-style metal doors close and the tops of our opponents' heads going down. We waited impatiently for the elevator to come back up. I was still standing at the check out desk when we saw the tail lights of Sarah's cab as it pulled away from the curb. "Get a cab quick," I told Lois.

Sarah and her copilot had the advantage at the airport. Since both of them were licensed pilots, one could go file the flight plans while the other went to get the airplane. Lois was an excellent copilot, but she was not licensed, so I had to do both jobs. Sarah was sitting in front of the time clock when I pulled up. As soon as the clock ticked off another minute, Lois punched it. We were two minutes behind them. I told a reporter later that it was because we stopped to put on our lipstick.

In the end, that slight delay worked in our favor. When Sarah reached the Mississippi River, she ran into a big thunderstorm and had to detour around it. As a result, she was forced to land at the next stop, Jackson, Mississippi. When I got there, there was an opening in the storm and I got through and made it all the way to the second stop down the way in Macon, Georgia. That put us one stop ahead of her. Just that minute or two had made all the difference. Macon was a "must" stop, but our three-minute stop there set a record for the shortest stop in the history of the Derby at that time. We stopped just long enough to punch in and out.

We finished the race one hour and seventeen minutes ahead of Sarah's team. The race had taken just under twenty-four hours, including the overnight stop in Tyler, Texas. As expected, we didn't win, but did we ever have fun! All the hoopla at the end of the race, the band, the roses, the television interviews, had been planned for the hometown girls. When we saw the headline the next day, "Indiana Fliers First to Land," we knew it was not the one the *Charleston Evening Post* had planned on. Even the winners of the race didn't get the publicity we got. I'm sure they were consoled, of course, by the eight hundred dollars cash they received. When we landed back in Fort Wayne, George's sons presented us with orchids. Our families were there to greet us. "Well, George," Morris joked as George looked over his plane, "it looks like it's all in one piece."

I smiled. "You didn't expect it to get scratched. Did you?"

(Below is a copy of our expenses for the 1958 Powder Puff Race.)

INVOICE

July 16, 1958

Gas and oil	$141.60
Hotels	$186.67
Taxis	$ 18.25
Meals	$ 46.00
Repair on J-35	$ 4.50
Entry fee	$ 25.00
Physical	$ 12.50
NAA license	$ 2.00

Registration fee	$ 20.00
Extra help at house	$ 50.00
Telephone	$ 18.00
Periodic plane inspection	$ 50.00
Special training	$ 25.00
Painting number on plane	$ 15.00
Supplies, maps, computers	$ 30.00
Total	$644.52

There were 14 sponsors.
Thus each sponsor's share is $ 46.00

✈

Race With The Sun

In the past I always had to hustle up a plane to fly in the race. The one I fly now is a club air plane. Morris and I own it with another couple and ten other members. I ride with every non-member who wants to fly it, and if that new person wants to become a member, I say, "This plane will be off the line for the month of June because this is the airplane I race." No one has ever objected. Maybe they like to tell people that they fly a plane that is used for racing.

There is always a certain amount of tension involved in securing a plane, but I remember one time in particular. It was 1959 and I went to George Bailey again to ask for an airplane to fly in the Powder Puff. I had been doing some work for him, flying airplanes over to Dayton, Ohio, when they needed work done on them. In addition, whenever he needed someone checked out on a plane, he asked me to do it. I had made some trips for him in a K-Bonanza and had decided that was the plane I wanted for the race. Now when I get into an airplane, my WASP training comes into play. I like to check it out. I go all around it and check the tires, the wings, the prop, the engine. Then I make sure all the paperwork is in order. When I take it up, I like to see what it will do. The Bonanza, I found, was slow and I had told George that on more than one occasion. "You just don't know how to fly it," he would say. Then I'd find out later from his secretary that as soon as I left his office, he would be on the phone to Dayton. He would then fly the plane down there and have it checked out. When he got it back, he would have me take it out again. I think he knew it was slow for a Bonanza; he just didn't want to admit I was right. Finally, he got fed up with it and two or three days before I was to leave for the race, he dropped a bomb: "The airplane is sold, so you're not going to be able to fly it for the race."

"What am I going to do?" I asked, dumfounded.

"Do you want to call another dealer?" he asked.

Finding an airplane on such short notice wasn't going to be easy, especially since I needed one that was the same make and model. The Bonanza had already been registered and cleared to fly so I couldn't change. I was a nervous wreck. I called Bevel Howard, the Beech dealer in Charleston, and several other Beech dealers, but nobody had a K-Bonanza. Finally I said to George, "Maybe Olive Ann can do something for me." Going directly to the owner of Beechcraft was going to be a long shot, but I was desperate.

"Call her," he said, handing me the number.

I dialed and waited. "They're calling her to the phone," I whispered.

George straightened. "That's impossible. She's in Hawaii."

I glared at him. "Then why did you tell me . . .?" Then Olive Ann was on the phone. "This is Margaret Ringenberg," I told her, unsure that she would remember me from our one brief encounter. I explained my predicament.

"We do not do that!" she exploded. Her tone was icy as she explained her position: if she were to lend me a plane and then I didn't win, it would make Beechcraft look bad. I wanted to cry.

"Well, I just thought I'd try," I said.

I was about to hang up when she said, "Wait, Margaret. Let me call you back. How long will you be there?"

"Until you call." Twenty minutes dragged by. The phone rang.

"All right, Margaret, I've got a plane for you," Olive Ann said. There was one small problem however; the plane was out on the East Coast. Normally I would fly the plane to the starting line of the race so I could get a feel for it, but the race was starting in Lawrence, Massachusetts, so I wasn't going to have much of a chance to fly it before the race. The airplane had to have an annual inspection, have the numbers put on, and everything had to be cleared. Olive Ann arranged for the person with the plane to meet us in Boston. Then he was going to ride with me to Lawrence so I could be cleared for insurance purposes. I called the airport and got a commercial flight for Lois and myself to Cleveland, where we had to change planes to New York. It was early the next morning before we arrived in Boston. We got into the Bonanza and I flew over to another airport and did a couple of landings. The next stop was the Beech shop in Boston where they did all the work and put on the number. Numbers are assigned in the order pilots register for the race. I was number 4 that year. The numbers are taped on and, because there is less wind resistance with a one digit number, serious racers strive to get a low number.

Meanwhile, I called race headquarters and asked for an extension. "I've got another K," I told Betty Gillies, the chairwoman of the board. "But I may be a little late." Without hesitation, she gave me a one-hour extension, although, as it turned out, I made the original deadline anyway. When I got up to Lawrence, all ready to go, Betty called me into her office.

"Margaret, what is your intention?" she asked.

"I want to go all the way in one day and break a record," I answered. I had just told Olive Ann Beech the same thing.

"I suspected something like that," Betty said. There are no regulations that say a pilot can't complete the race in one day, but it's not the way to win the race. I knew that, but my mind was set on giving it a try. "We were going to have people with time clocks only as far as Fargo the first day," Betty continued. "We'll put some more people out there all the way."

Lois Laymon was my copilot again that year. Takeoff was scheduled for 0900 (9 a.m.) on Saturday, July 4. We were the fourth plane in the air. Four hours, seventeen minutes and eleven seconds later we taxied into the Municipal Airport at Kokomo, Indiana. Morris and the kids, as well as George Bailey, were there to meet us. The race program listed George and "fourteen civic-minded citizens of Fort Wayne" as my sponsors. We made the front page of the Kokomo paper. George had come bearing oxygen bottle and masks since going out we hadn't been able to take the things we needed. The traditional greeting by city officials ate up fifteen precious minutes as we accepted gifts of charm bracelets and letter openers from the chairman of the Chamber of Commerce. We were anxious to be off.

"It's getting on," George said, trying to hurry things along.

"I have to check weather," I said.

"I checked weather and filed your flight plan," he said. "Get going." We took off and just west of Chicago, we hit the worst weather front I have ever seen. It was terrible! Minutes, then hours, slipped away as we bucked stiff headwinds, thunderstorms, even a tornado. The plane was bouncing all over the place, and I was seriously questioning George's source of weather information. Four hours and twenty-five minutes later, we set down in Fargo, North Dakota, in a spray of water, brakes squealing. Lois made a mad dash for the time clock. It took twenty-six minutes to refuel, grab a cup of coffee, file flight plans and shake hands with more city officials before we wheeled to the flight line and headed for Helena, Montana.

Once again foul weather was our undoing. I had thought we could make Helena, the next required stop, by 7:45 p.m. but headwinds slowed us down so much and caused us to use so much more gas, that we had to make an unscheduled fourteen-minute stop in Miles City, Montana, before crossing the Rockies. I was getting worried. We had filed our flight plan at 6:36 p.m. Under normal flying conditions it would take about two hours to reach Helena. Barring any problems, that would put us in Helena at 8:36 p.m. If we failed to check in at Helena before the official 8:24 sunset, our chances for glory would vanish in disqualification.

There was no hope now of completing the race in one day, but we left Miles City, determined to beat the clock. About halfway to Helena, we ran into headwinds again. Crossing time zones, it was becoming difficult to keep track of the time. When we crossed the Continental Divide I could still see the sun, but the shadows in the valleys were growing long. Suddenly I had contact with the unicom at Helena down in a valley. It was not a controlled field, meaning it had no tower, and I was heading straight for a runway. They had turned on the lights to give us a clearer target. I called for airport advisory.

"Observe a right traffic pattern," a voice told us. Right? Ordinarily traffic patterns were left and I had started for a left. I swung the plane around so quickly that Lois blacked out for a moment. I grabbed the mike.

"I'm on downwind. . .I'm on crosswind. . .

I'm on final." I was still going too fast to drop my gear. Finally when I was almost to the fence, I chopped the power, pulled the nose up, dropped the gear, and came in for a landing. I was still a good half mile from the finish line. Ignoring the little "Follow Me" truck, I passed it and taxied up the runway at a speed better suited for takeoff than landing. About fifty feet from the final white line, I put on the brakes, pulled the mixture, and the prop stopped. The nose wheel came to a stop about three feet from the line. As soon as the plane came to a complete stop, Lois leaped from the plane and raced to the clock. I agonized as my very deliberate sister-in-law carefully put the card in the time clock. I would have shoved it in just as fast as I could. Even the timing officials cheered as the log was stamped. Horns started honking all over the airport. It was 8:22 p.m. We had raced with the sun and won — by two minutes.

I opened the door and the first person I saw was a girl who had been in WASP training with me at Sweetwater. "Marjorie Logan!" I called, surprising her and myself that I remembered her name. When I started the plane again to take it to the parking area, I was so exhausted I could hardly maneuver. But a great treat awaited me at the hotel. I discovered "magic fingers." I had to put a quarter in the bed and give it a try.

We finished the race at 5:33 a.m. the next day, twelve hours ahead of the second plane. In doing so we had come within an hour and a half of completing the race in one day, although we did set a record for the longest one-day flight in the history of the race.

I don't know why we were surprised when

we arrived at Spokane to discover that no one was there. We watched as the voice in the tower materialized and rushed to the time clock. He was the entire welcoming committee. There had been some kind of upset with the volunteers at the race terminus and even the news media had decided to stay away. We caught a ride to the hotel and there we sat. We didn't even have a change of clothes. Lois couldn't sit still. "Do you want me to take your dress down and wash it?" she asked. She put on her swimsuit and grabbing our clothes, went down to the washer. When she got back, we borrowed an iron and pressed our dresses. Then we sat some more. We both jumped when the phone rang. It was the desk clerk. "There's a photographer down here who wants some pictures. Would it be possible for you to come down?"

I smiled at Lois. "We'd be happy to."

"Have you had breakfast yet?" the photographer asked when we met him.

"Not yet."

"Maybe instead of taking the pictures here, we could take them by the airplane," he suggested. "Would you mind riding out to the airport? There's a restaurant on the way. Would you like to stop and eat?" It wasn't as if we had anything else to do. There, while we were eating, he got on his walkie-talkie and talked to several people. By the time we reached the airport there were police and all kinds of people there. We had our pictures taken and were thrilled with the attention.

But. . . we didn't win. Gambling on the weather and trying to set a record had cost us the race. It had taken us fifteen hours and one minute to cover the 2,470-mile course from Lawrence,

Massachusetts, to Spokane, Washington. The Bonanza that could easily do 185 miles per hour had been reduced to a mere 164. We were thirtieth in a field of forty-five entries who had finished the race. The winners, Aileen Saunders and Jerelyn Cassell of California, had waited out the weather and finished three days later with an average speed of 111.52 miles per hour, some nine points better than par for their Cessna 172. To this day, no one who has crossed the finish line first has ever won the race, but I had to try, didn't I?

"The north suburban area's flying duo, Mrs. Margaret Ringenberg and Mrs. Lois Laymon, flew home from Spokane, Washington, Sunday with an average speed that would have won the Powder Puff Derby hands down. They covered the distance from Spokane to Baer Field in only eight hours and twenty-eight minutes, for an average speed of well over 200 miles per hour."— Excerpt from Suburban Life, Fort Wayne, Indiana, July 16, 1959

✈

The Yellow-Tired Champ

Two years in a row, I had crossed the finish line first, but out of the money. In 1960 I promised the race organizers and myself that I wasn't going to try that again. Let someone else get the publicity; I was looking for a win. I decided to change my strategy. Instead of the fastest plane in the race like the year before, I chose the slowest, a 90-horsepower Champion. Failing in my attempt to finish the race in one day, I planned to take the full four days allotted if necessary and make every stop. That way I hoped to take advantage of tailwinds, avoid thunderstorms, and pick up some time. Another way to cut precious minutes off the time is to make sure the airplane is clean and waxed. But that year, my passion for a shiny airplane proved to be my undoing.

One of our sponsors that year was Gehrig Rubber Manufacturing Company of Portland, Indiana. They made tires for antique cars, and the owner, Bob Gehrig, had an idea to make colored tires for the airplane. At every stop we planned to show them off and get some publicity for the company. When Bob realized there wasn't enough time to have the tires drop-tested and certified by the FAA, he decided he would have to get a pair of tires and retread them. He did them in gold and they were beautiful . . . until he put them in the heat treatment. We thought we were going to be the first to enter the race with khaki-colored tires! Bob assured us he would try another method and have the tires shipped to us in California. He was true to his word and our plane was soon being dubbed "The Yellow-tired Champ."

The race began in Torrance, California, and ended in Wilmington, Delaware. How great it would be to win there, where I had been stationed in the WASP! Flying such a slow plane was a big change from the previous year, but we knew with the handicap system it was possible for the slowest plane to win. We were counting on our strategy, but since the scoring would not be announced until the end when everyone had finished, it was impossible to know where we stood at each stop. It wasn't until the next to the last stop in Johnson City, Tennessee, that we realized we weren't doing well at all. There, a mechanic pointed out that, unlike other airplanes that had metal bodies, this Champion had a fabric-covered body. Instead of increasing our speed as we had hoped, the coating of wax had collected dirt and dust, slowing us down all the way. The mechanic estimated that we had lost at least ten miles per hour. We worked frantically to wash off as much as we could, but the damage had been done. When the race ended, we had finished in fifty-fourth place, our worst finish yet.

Not only was I discouraged, I was humiliated. People back home at Smith Field told Bob we had ruined his plane. "How are you going to get that stuff off?" they asked. "That plane will never be any good again. He never should have let you fly it." I felt terrible. Bob, on the other hand, didn't seem to be all that upset. The plane was not ruined, he assured me, and with several washings we did eventually get the wax off. As it turned out, it may not have been the wax that defeated us after all. The airplane was new and Bob had forgotten to tell us that it had break-in oil in it. By the time I had flown it to California for the start, it needed an oil change. I asked the shop to change the oil and they unwittingly put in regular oil. As I flew, a kind of lacquer had formed on the cylinders, adding friction and cutting the horsepower even more.

Whatever the reason, it was an ill-fated race, and I was in no mood to fly that plane again when Bob approached me a few months later and asked me to fly the S.M.A.L.L. race. The Southern Michigan All Lady Lark is a proficiency race in which the pilot must predict, before knowing the course, how much fuel will be consumed and at what average speed the plane will travel. I didn't want to do it. "Hey, you flew it in the Powder Puff and you had some problems," Bob said. "This is a different race. I have confidence in you." It was my confidence that worried me.

I decided to fly it solo. Maybe I didn't want to embarrass another copilot by making a poor showing again. My choice of a plain black dress to wear in the race, reflected my mood. The race, a one hundred eighty-mile triangular course that began and ended in Muskegon, Michigan, took just under two hours to complete. My watch didn't even have a second hand, so I had no idea how I was doing for time. I didn't bother to change out of my black dress before attending the awards banquet that evening. What was the point? I certainly wasn't going to win. When they started announcing the places beginning with number twenty-four, I was barely listening. But when they got to number four and my name had still not been called, I began to take notice. "And in first place with an average speed of ninety-seven miles per hour, Margaret Ringenberg!" I had missed my fuel consumption by only .0187 gallons and my speed by 1.5 miles per hour. As I had my picture taken with the one-hundred-year-old trophy, I was suddenly very conscious of the rumpled black dress I wore. Only months earlier I had flown my worst race in that plane, and now I had won the first race of my career in it. I will always be grateful to Bob Gehrig for pushing me into that race and to the little "Yellow-tired Champ" that helped me win it.

ANOTHER VOICE:

Marsha Wright

I flew two transcontinental races with Mom. She had a wonderful time introducing me to people and showing me the sights. I love to sightsee and was delighted with it all. The only boring part was the "hangar flying." It seemed that all these women could talk about was airplanes! During the race, there was so little to see from our altitude that sometimes I would fall asleep with my finger on the map. I have since learned that when we would cross the map and go on to the next one, Mom would slip it under my finger. I would wake up later and be pleased to be right on course! Since she later flew the race solo, I know she didn't need me for the flying. I think my most important role was telling her when she needed lipstick or if her slip was showing.

✈

Winning Isn't Every-thing

After the 1958 Powder Puff I was quoted as saying, "I teach flying to a few students, but otherwise I'm a housewife. I wash dishes and mop floors for a living." Now almost forty years later, I still teach flying to a few students, but someone else mops my floors these days. But whether I call myself a housewife, a corporate pilot, or an air racer, I've had the opportunity to meet a lot of interesting people I wouldn't have met if not for flying.

In 1969 when the race ended in Washington D.C., Senator Barry Goldwater, who had been a member of the Ferrying Division when I was, presented the trophies. I had my picture taken with all the politicians from Indiana — Vance

Hartke, E. Ross Adair, Birch Bayh. I even had tea at the White House that year. Mrs. Nixon was the hostess. Another year, actor Martin Milner was the honorary starter of the race. I snapped his picture. I had my picture taken with country music star Roy Clark, but there are others, not necessarily famous, who stick in my mind.

In 1978, I was flying the Classic from Las Vegas, Nevada, to Destin-Fort Walton Beach, Florida. The race that year was sponsored by Hughes Airwest, the company that carried the name of multi-millionaire, Howard Hughes. For a city to get the privilege of hosting the race, large sums of money were put up by a sponsor, since it would generate considerable publicity for the city and its airport. At the start and finish of a race, there is a party for the competitors that usually includes a reception line of city officials and prominent citizens. As I passed along the line that year, one of the ladies in the line asked, "Where's your other half?" She was referring to the fact that all the pilots and copilots were dressed in matching outfits.

"I'm flying solo," I told her.

"Oh? What are you flying?" she asked.

"A Mooney."

She looked at me strangely. "What is a Mooney?" I explained that it was an airplane that appeared to have its tail on backwards. She laughed and I moved on down the line. I didn't know who she was, and frankly I didn't give it another thought as the race continued. At the end of the race, I was the second one to cross the finish line. Early in the morning as I taxied up to the terminal, I spotted a big limousine. Who

185

should step out of that enormous car, but the lady I had talked to back in Las Vegas. Now I was intrigued. She was about seventy years old, very short, and had one of those big beehive hairdos. I could hardly have missed her. She got out, looked at me and the airplane and said, "You do have your tail on backwards." I still did not know who she was, but a person who is at both the start and finish of the race and arrives in a limo must be someone. "We heard on the radio that you were coming in," she told us. "So we came right out." She and her husband were going to drive me and my two competitors into town. I unloaded, took the plane to impound, and turned in my key. This procedure is a safeguard against anyone tampering with the airplane. Our hosts picked us up and drove us to the condominiums where we would be staying.

I had a slight problem. The other two teams with whom I was to share a condo had not come in yet. The weather had closed in and they were not expected for a couple of days. I had flown the race solo, but I was not prepared to pay for the condo alone. I went to the desk. "I'm not registered to come in for another two days," I explained. "Do you have a back room or someplace I can stay until the other two teams arrive?" Thoughts of my WASP days when I could sleep between train cars, came to mind. Suddenly, my hostess spoke up.

"You're not going to do that," she said. "We have an extra bedroom in our condo and you can join us." I really didn't care where I stayed as long as I had a place, so I agreed. She convinced me to join her and her husband for breakfast and we went down to the clubroom. I excused myself for a minute so I could call Morris and tell him I had arrived. There were several waitresses standing in the serving station near the pay phone. "Do you know who that lady is over there with her hair piled high on her head?" I asked them. It had occurred to me that if I was going to spend the night with them, it might be a good idea to know who they were.

"You mean you don't know who you're eating with?" The waitresses looked at each other and laughed.

"No."

"That is Nadine Hensley. She used to be Howard Hughes's personal secretary." I told myself that next time I should pay a little more attention to the people at the race as well as the weather and my airplane. At that time, the military in Fort Walton Beach was negotiating to get Howard Hughes' airplane, "The Spruce Goose." They had invited the Hensleys to the officers' club for dinner. "There will be five us ," she told them, gesturing to me and the other two pilots.

"Oh, I can't go like this," I protested. "These are the clothes I was wearing when I left Las Vegas."

"You're fine as you are," she said. "And we insist."

When everyone crossed the finish line a day or two later and the scores were tallied, I finished in a disappointing twenty-seventh place. On the other hand, the winner didn't have dinner at the Officers' Club with Howard Hughes's secretary.

Before the start of the 1970 Powder Puff in Monterey, California, I saw a woman sitting alone.

187

My copilot, Mary Weaver, and I introduced our-selves to her and asked if she was flying the race solo. "No, I'm the honorary starter," she said, tell-ing us her name was Trudy Cooper. We asked her to join us for lunch. "You're so lucky to go as copi-lot," she told Mary. "I would love to be in the Pow-der Puff once."

Mary and I went on to have a good race that year, although we didn't place. We began making plans to give it another try the next year. We stayed in contact through the year, but just before we were to send our entry in, Mary got a chance to travel around the world on a freighter. I needed a copilot.

I thought of Trudy Cooper, who had men-tioned that she had a private license and instru-ment ticket, but I had no idea how to contact her. She was from the Houston area, but I did not have an address or phone number. Later when I flew Jim Kelly of Fort Wayne to Washington on busi-ness, I mentioned my dilemma. He promised to get the address. When I picked him up he had it, and I scribbled off a note to Trudy, saying that if she was interested in being my copilot, I needed to know in five days. Two days later, she called with an enthusiastic "Yes!" We met in Indianapo-lis to look for a sponsor, and I was able to get an airplane from Walt Lupke. The Commanche, with retractable gear, had variable pitch meaning that the prop could change to give more speed, in this case up to 80 miles per hour. When we sent in our entry, the press got hold of the news that I was going to fly the race with the wife of retired astro-naut Gordon Cooper! A reporter called and wanted to come to my house for an interview so I set a time. Then unexpectedly, Jim Kelly asked me to fly him to French Lick, Indiana. He had planned on using our Mooney to fly himself, but at the last minute decided the weather was not to his liking.

I made the trip to southern Indiana and back in good time and was hurrying home from the airport to meet the reporter when I met a car on a curve near my home. The other driver was taking his half out of the middle. I swerved sharply, rolling my car on to its side, slid across the wet pavement and hit a cement bridge abutment. I was thrown from the car and landed in a ditch. The first people to come along were a man and woman with a little girl. They were on their way home from fishing in the nearby river when they witnessed the accident. The man ran down to check on me and went to call an ambulance. After a few minutes, I got up and walked over to their car. The woman was hysterical. She had seen my wig go flying when I was thrown from the car and thought it was my head! Reassuring her that my head was still attached, I asked for something to wipe my bleeding chin, and she handed me a washrag. I grimaced, suspecting it was the same rag they had used to wipe their fishy hands, but what could I do?

The local paramedics, who lived in my community, came and took me to the hospital, and I asked them afterward to go by my house and tell the reporter what had happened. When X-rays revealed I had a couple of broken ribs, they taped me up, stitched my chin and lip and released me. I was sore the next day, but up and around. Two days later I was scheduled to go back and get Mr. Kelly. Morris went with me to untie and line check

check the airplane. I was concerned about whether I could get the landing gear up, due to my sore ribs, but I knew that once I picked up Jim, he could fly back. The look on his face when he saw my face was priceless.

My main concern was that the accident had slowed down our preparations for the Powder Puff, which was only a few weeks away. Trudy and I were doing all our planning on the phone. Then one evening she called and suggested we meet at her house in Texas. It would give me a few extra days to rest before the race. "She invited me to her house," I told Morris when I got off the phone.

"You should go," he said. "We'll come up with the money for gas." So I went to Houston. We had a good time and I had the opportunity to meet her children. When we took off for the race, we flew the course backwards from Baton Rouge to the start at Calgary, checking out the airports along the way. As soon as we got to the hotel, there was a message for Trudy from a local school, asking her to ring the bell for the last day of classes. The next day when we went down to the lobby, the press swarmed Trudy. They started asking her questions and I could see that she didn't know what they were talking about. She played it cool, saying, "I'd like to have more time to think about it before making a statement." We got away and back upstairs before we learned that three Soviet cosmonauts had died on their return to earth after setting a record for twenty-four days in space.

The 1971 Powder Puff proved to be an interesting race. One hundred forty-four planes took off from Calgary, including one with a monkey named Cherie for a copilot. Since the rules prohibited only men from flying the race, I think after that they had to specify that all participants also had to be human! There was a little trouble when Cherie locked herself in the bathroom of her hotel room and a locksmith had to be called to remove the door.

It was fun having Trudy as my copilot. The news people dogged her every step, but she was always gracious. I was impressed at how she handled herself, referring the reporters to me whenever they asked questions about the race or airplane. "Margaret is in command," she would say. Actually, it was ironic that the media seemed to focus on the fact that Trudy was *Mrs.* Gordon Cooper, when in reality she had earned her private license before her husband had earned his. Ironically, the astronaut who had spent eight days aboard Gemini V in 1965 may have owed much of his interest in flying to her.

We were the third plane to land in Baton Rouge. While we didn't win the race, we did win two leg prizes. The hotel in Baton Rouge was a rare experience too. It had gone bankrupt prior to the race, but for the benefit of the Powder Puff, staff had been brought in to work the desk and switchboard. We had nice rooms, but were unable to use the phone because of the mixed-up switchboard. Then, when we attempted to check out, we were told our bill had already been paid. We knew we hadn't paid for it so we told them to contact us when they discovered their error. About a week later, I got a letter from the hotel with a refund for our room! No wonder they had gone bankrupt.

Then there was the time we got to Corpus

Christi, Texas, a day early for the 1993 race. My copilot, Lois Feigenbaum, and I spent the night in a hotel and were back at the airport early the next morning to work on our plane. When we noticed all the news photographers milling around, looking for Pauline Glasson, who was heading up the race, we sat back to watch the hubbub. Pauline, who was eighty-three years old, was also flying the race, so at only seventy-three, I felt like quite the youngster. We looked up when a well-dressed woman approached us, asking, "Does anyone besides me want to get away from this airport?"

"Yes," we answered, ready to get out of the Texas sun. We had finished cleaning the plane and were anxious to get back to the hotel and get ourselves cleaned up. She took us to her car, which was a brand-new Cadillac. It was beautiful, but better yet, it was air-conditioned. We weren't sure if she was a pilot or just assigned to drive us so I asked, "Are you going to fly in the race?"

"Oh, no. I've had all the racing I can take for this year," she answered.

"I could never get tired of racing," I said.

"If you had to sit in Indianapolis for two months like I did, you'd be tired of racing too," she answered. Indianapolis? There was common ground. I was an avid Indy 500 fan and never missed the race. I pointed out that A.J. Foyt and I had started racing the same year.

When I found out she actually knew A.J., I said, "Will you tell him I'm not a bit happy that he retired?" She laughed. When I asked if she got up to the 500 often, she told me that not only did she get to the 500, she and her husband owned two cars and Jeff Andretti was their driver. Now I was really impressed. "Sorry," I said. "But I'm rooting for Mario because he's number six and I'm number six this year." Before I knew it we were deep in conversation about the race and what kind of wax they used on the cars. We had been driving for some time before she realized she had made a wrong turn back at the airport and was going away from the hotel. We were all quite well acquainted by the time we arrived.

At the takeoff banquet, she introduced all the girls, and when she got to us she said, "And here is team number six. We are the best of friends." She announced our names, made a few jokes and had her picture taken with us. When we went back to our seats, I noticed her purse, a cute little leather bag with a zipper, lying on the table. I don't know what came over me, but I unzipped the purse and started to stuff all the little sugar packets from the table into it. "Here, put these in too," Lois said shoving some more toward me. I didn't realize anyone else was watching us until one of several important-looking men at the next table, said, "Hey, it's not full yet. Put these in too," and they handed over all the sugar packets from their table. We stuffed them in, zipped the purse, and put it back. When she finished speaking, she came back to the table and took off her glasses. She started talking, all the while trying to cram her glasses into her purse. She finally succeeded and went right on talking, while we stifled giggles. The next morning I asked her if she had enough sugar for her cereal. "Oh, you!" she said, laughing. "Last night I went to get my glasses out of my purse, and when I dumped it out on the table all these sugar packets fell out. Someone asked me what I was doing with all of them and I didn't know."

When the race ended a few days later in Rhode Island, I didn't win. I finished in second place, but then the winner didn't get an invitation to watch the Indy 500 from the pit area!

ANOTHER VOICE:

Lois Feigenbaum
(COPILOT AND FRIEND)

Margaret and I have known each other for many years. In 1971, my pregnant daughter and I flew the Powder Puff Derby, as did Margaret and Trudy Cooper. We became closer friends during that race when we all went shopping in Canada for an English pram for my future grandchild. We really had fun together.

Margaret and I started racing together in the 1991 Air Race Classic and have raced together ever since. As good a pilot as I feel I am (I have an ATP), she can fly rings around me. Margaret is the best pilot I have ever flown with and I am very particular with whom I fly. On one occasion while flying one of the races, we were doing so well that we thought we were in first place. We had been flying at 13,500 feet in Margaret's Piper Cherokee 160C and the winds were not as forecast. We decided to descend and fly "on the deck," then found we were using more fuel than anticipated. Margaret said, "Do we have enough fuel to make the next stop?"

I did some calculating and said, "I'm not sure; I think so."

"What should we do?" We calculated again and decided, as experienced flight instructors, when in doubt, choose on the side of safety. We landed, refueled, and flew to the next stop. At the end of the race we placed 5th overall.

In the 1997 Air Race Classic we flew an airplane that had a terrible handicap, and we knew that we had no chance whatsoever to place in the top ten. It was a choice to fly the race for the camaraderie or stay home. We decided to fly the race for the "fun of it," and as expected did not place in the top ten -- something that is uncommon for Margaret.

Mike Ringenberg
(SON)

The summer I graduated from high school, Mom planned to fly the Powder Puff with a copilot from California. She would have to fly the plane from Indiana to California alone so Mom invited me to ride with her. Of course, I jumped at the chance. We left Baer Field early in the morning and along the way, she taught me to follow the aviation charts. I enjoyed looking out the window and watching the terrain below. After an overnight in Salt Lake City, we continued on the next morning and landed at the airport in Santa Monica.

Two days later, after I did some sightseeing, Mom took me to the Los Angeles airport to catch a commercial flight. Even though I had flown with my mom many times, I had only flown on an airliner once before when I was three and my parents took my sister and me to visit my grandparents who were missionaries in Jamaica. So my trip back from LA, including a stop in Denver to change planes, was a memorable experience for me.

✈

. . .But Neither is Losing

here is only one way to win the transcontinental race: score the most points by flying
over the handicapped speed of the airplane.
There are a lot of ways not to win. I can describe
several. When I flew into San Diego for the start
of the 1969 Powder Puff Derby, I discovered a gauge
that wasn't working properly. I recall the mechanic
fixing something up under the panel, and we were
on our way. We didn't have much in the way of
navigational aids, so we had to rely on mountain
peaks for our bearings. We had communication;
we could talk on the radio, but we didn't realize
that our omni headings were inaccurate. Om-
nirange is a network of very high frequency radio
signals that are emitted simultaneously in all di-

196

rections from a transmitting station. These enable a pilot to plot her bearings from the station. We tried following it, but it did not match up with the ground track we were on.

"You take over while I see what I can find," I said to Evelyn Bowyer, my copilot. I turned around and got down under the panel while she flew.

"Can you see anything, Margaret?" she asked.

"No. We're going to have to turn back and look for something visual." Finally we found a railroad track and followed it into Salt Lake City. On the ground I had our situation checked. It turned out that the first person who had fixed the gauge back in California had noticed that something under the panel was unplugged so he plugged it in. Unfortuantely for us, it wasn't supposed to be plugged in and caused the omni heads to short out. Once we unplugged it, everything worked fine, but it cost us valuable time and a shot at first place.

The 1972 Powder Puff started in San Mateo County, California, and ended in Tom's River, New Jersey. I made the first stop in Winnemucca, Nevada. Because there is always a mob of airplanes at the first stop of any race, I had to wait my turn to refuel. The time on the ground was not counting against us, but everyone, of course, was anxious to get going. Winnemucca is located at a fairly high altitude so the procedure for starting an airplane would be different than at low altitudes. I got refueled, got back into the plane and followed the correct procedure, but it seemed that the engine just wasn't turning over fast enough. Finally it caught and we were off.

Once over the mountains, I tried to use the VOR radios, but they would come on and go out. "We're just not high enough to pick up the signal," I told my copilot, Ruth Christen. "We'll be able to pick up the signal when we get over Great Salt Lake." I tried to call Ogden, Utah, but they didn't answer. Once in awhile I could pick them up talking to someone else, but obviously they could not hear me. Suddenly I noticed that my alternator gauge was sitting on zero! I was running everything out of the battery. The Mooney has a hand gear so I wasn't worried about that, but I could not go in and land without a clearance which I could not get without radio contact. The only thing to do was fly over the airport and circle. Eventually they would give me a green light from the light gun and I would be cleared to land. It worked, but it took so-o-o long. When I got on the ground, I had somebody fix the problem, as I watched first place slip away again.

The 1976 Powder Puff was supposed to be the last, due to rising costs and increased air traffic. We were all saddened at the end of an era. Then the Smithsonian Institute pointed out that by flying one more race, it would make an even thirty years. The new Air Race Classic had already been organized, so a Powder Puff Commemorative Race was planned. The race or "pilgrimage" was to start in Palm Springs, California, the site of the first Powder Puff, and end in Tampa, Florida. We were assigned questions to answer at each leg of the race, like about what you see at a certain latitude and longitude, and what hotel chain is in a particular section of the map. It was supposed to be fun, but when I couldn't find the silly hotel chain it really blew my mind. It happened to be in Locuenta, New Mexico, and the hotel we were to locate was the Locuenta Hotel. The girls from California and the West had the advantage, since we did not have those hotels in the Midwest and did not know the logo.

Another thing I did wrong was fly a fast plane. The slower the plane, the better the chance of finding all the things. I also realized that if there had been more than two of us in the plane, we could have researched things better. What's that they say about twenty-twenty hindsight? I guess the Powder Puff Derby couldn't end without a twist. One of the last stops was in Thomasville, Georgia. There was a big golf tournament taking place there and most of the hotels were filled. Because not many of the planes had planned to stop there, the organizers had not thought it would be a problem. Then the weather closed in and everybody had to stop. We stayed in people's houses, and some of the women even stayed at an undertakers!

I lost the Indiana F.A.I.R. proficiency race in 1976 too. As in all proficiency races, I had tried to figure my time down to the second for each leg. My goal then was to fly at a speed and on a course that would bring me over the finish line at just the right instant, as close to my estimate as possible. Lots of things can go wrong in a proficiency race. Winds can slow the plane down or push it too fast. A pilot can miss an airport and have to turn back, or even get lost. Watches can stop, leaving the pilot no way to count seconds. Just to be sure, I had taken three watches. One worked. I was disappointed when I lost. It was the first time in sixteen years that I hadn't taken a trophy home. My copilot, Nancy Romero, was sure she was a jinx, but in reality it was a new engine cylinder that had been my undoing. I had just had the cylinder replaced the day before, and it simply did not give me the performance I expected. Such a little thing.

We encountered ice in the mountains in 1979. Being from the flat Midwest, I sometimes get uneasy flying over the mountains. We never flew higher than 4,000 feet that year and had to go twenty miles off course at one time to avoid bad weather. Even then we were grounded for two days in Walla Walla, Washington, due to the weather, in spite of the fact that the weather forecaster had given the go-ahead. I celebrated my birthday there that year on the race by finding out I was in second place at that point. I held that place to the end of the race, finishing only three miles per hour behind the winner, Marion Jayne.

I was headed for the 1993 Air Race Classic in Corpus Christi, Texas, when I had a fuel pump go out. I had to stop in St. Louis to get one. I got to the start and checked into a hotel. The next morning I went out to the airport to clean up the plane. During my inspection, race officials went over my paperwork and discovered that we had the wrong dates on the insurance papers. It was Friday at three in the afternoon when I called my insurance representative in Columbus, Ohio. "No way I can get it to you today," he said. "I'll have to call Maryland and have them go over the paperwork and fax it to me. The place closes in an hour."

"If they don't get it today, I'll have to wait until Monday," I protested. "The race starts Tuesday and I can't take off without papers."

"I'll do what I can," he promised. I went back to the hotel. There was nothing to do but wait. It wasn't easy. I had flown every race since 1957. I just couldn't miss this one over paperwork. Saturday, I ran out to the airport to check over the plane again. I had given the insurance company the fax number at the Beechcraft office, so I checked in there too. I've learned over the years not to have things delivered to the hotel. Morris used to send me telegrams, but I never seemed to get them. I explained about the fax.

"Oh, that came in just after you left," a clerk said. With that settled, I could relax a little. Another woman had a car so we decided to drive to San Padre Island.

"There's a hurricane coming," the man at the gate told us as we paid our four dollars. The sun was shining; it was a beautiful day. How could there be a hurricane coming? We took our time, saw the dunes, the unusual birds and animals, and went back to the hotel. The hurricane hit, as expected, during the night. We didn't even hear it. While the women staying on the south side of the hotel were stuffing towels around the doors and windows to keep the water out, we slept peacefully on the north side, oblivious to the storm.

It was a difficult race. The hurricane had unsettled the weather all along the race route, and we ran into one thunderstorm after another. Even so, I felt fairly confident about my chances. Being from the Midwest, I flew in bad weather all the time. In fact, I thought I did some of my best flying in the worst weather, but I wasn't going to admit it. During the race when one pilot asks another how she thinks she is doing, the answer is always the same: "Not very well." I was no different. I knew the thunderstorms were slowing me down, but I assumed they were doing the same to everyone else too. Unfortunately, there was one person it didn't affect quite so much: the winner. I came in second again. One thing I have learned over the years. Always expect the unexpected. No matter how much a pilot plans, when she is dealing with machines and weather conditions, anything can happen.

ANOTHER VOICE:

G. Michael Livingston

It has been obvious to me, since the first time I met Margaret, that she would rather fly than do almost anything. Although I couldn't fly the all-female Air Race Classic with her, I was often involved in the pre-race preparations. We spent a great deal of time making sure the plane was waxed to perfection, and then we would ferry the plane back and forth from the mechanic until she was satisfied that everything was in perfect running order. Being a detail person, she was always interested in technical things. Whenever either of us got a new avionics instrument like a Loran or GPS, she would spend hours trying to learn everything about it. I was never sure if it was because she just liked to fiddle with a new toy or if she wanted to reassure herself that she could use it in any situation. She wasn't happy until she mastered it.

I always enjoyed hearing about her racing adventures. One time she told me about a Powder Puff race in which she was flying through the Rocky Mountains. Because her plane could not maintain the necessary altitude to fly over the mountains, she had opted to follow a canyon. All of a sudden, she told me, there was a wall in front of her. The canyon was a dead-end! With only seconds to make a decision, she banked the plane into a steep dive, turned the plane around and went back the way she had come.

With Margaret there never seem to be problems, only potential problems. Impossible situations? Not to her. She just figures them out. She is always thinking ahead, always planning. One night, flying back from Illinois with her, we ran into a snowstorm somewhere over the Indiana-Illinois border. As the pilot I made the decision to get under it into clearer air as quickly as possible and I began a rapid descent. Very calmly, Margaret advised, "Don't do it so steeply because we might suck too much snow into the engine and stall it out." Trusting her intuition, I promptly changed the rate of descent to her recommendation.

Number Two is Number One

In 1988, after eleven tries, I finally won the Air Race Classic. Following the announcement, I joked, "I don't know what Morris will say when I tell him I want twelve diamonds." My gold Classic medallion had space for twenty stones to be mounted, but I always said I didn't want any until I finished first. My day had come.

I had placed second in 1986 and again in 1987, and while second was an excellent showing, I wasn't satisfied. I wanted to win. By lightening my load, I figured I could increase my speed by 1.2 miles per hour for every hundred pounds I got rid of. Since I was fairly certain I was not going to lose a hundred pounds myself by race time, I did the next best thing: I "lost" a copilot. I decided to fly the race solo.

Numbers for each plane are assigned in the order that registrations are received, so following my strategy, I sent mine in as soon as I got it. I was rewarded with the number "2." With thirty-two planes racing to small airfields like Laramie, Wyoming, I wanted to be able to get in and out as quickly as possible. My intention was to try to get to each of the refueling stops first. The race started well and I was feeling good about my chances. I was flying at 12,000 feet when somewhere between Winnemucca, Nevada, and Idaho Falls, Idaho, my engine quit. I was up in the mountains and there were up-drafts and down-drafts filled with moisture. My air intake was sucking up all that cold air and before I knew it the inside of the carburetor was coated with ice. It had been eighty degrees on the ground so I wasn't thinking about icing, but it was thirty-two degrees at that altitude. I was in radio contact with competitors Carolyn Pilaar and Gary Ann Wheeler of Greenville, South Carolina. As soon as I told them my engine quit, they offered to circle back in case I had to glide down. Immediately, I went into my emergency procedures. I put on the carburetor heat, which isn't a heater, but rather a little butterfly door on the air intake that can be closed, blocking out the cold air. The engine heat would melt the ice build-up. I switched gas tanks and switched on the fuel pump. In a matter of seconds, I had the engine restarted. "That's a good instructor," Carolyn teased. "You knew just what to do." I will never forget Carolyn and Gary's willingness to put my safety ahead of their desire to win.

I was making good time until I ran into a huge thunderstorm outside Kankakee, Illinois. I decided to climb to twelve or thirteen thousand feet to see if I could get out of it, and suddenly I had the most wonderful tailwind. When I landed and saw only the faster planes there ahead of me, I was delighted. I was still sitting in the plane when my closest competitors, Bonnie Gann and Shirley Zillig, came running out. "I can't believe it. I can't believe it," I kept repeating.

"You can't believe what?" Bonnie asked.

"I got in the jet stream! I made fantastic speeds!"

"Oh, shoot," Bonnie said, and suddenly I was aware that I was about to reveal my secrets to the competition. I tried to fluff it off, hoping they would think I was just exaggerating to unnerve them a little. A few minutes later, I slipped around the corner, filed my flight plan, gassed up and got out of there. The others were all still sitting because they had been told the weather would be better the next day. Bonnie and Shirley and several others were paying the same weather service that I was, C.L. Chandler out of Atlanta. They must have wondered what I was up to. They didn't know I had veered off course to miss the thunderstorm. As soon as I got into the air, I went back up to the same altitude, and I was right back in the jet stream! It was great. I was flying high in more ways than one when I crossed Indiana and headed for the finish line. There are those who do not like to pay for a weather service, but I feel it is a real advantage to have someone who can study the entire United States and give me information about headings, wind velocity and even recommend what time I should take off. A local flight service might tell me that I could expect helping winds the next day, but once I completed that leg, I might find myself fighting headwinds the rest of the way. I knew that if "my" weatherman sent me out in headwinds, he knew that at a certain point I would be able to pick up a tailwind that would more than make up for the time I had lost, but a little unexpected good luck didn't hurt either.

When I reached the finish line in Huntington, West Virginia, I knew I had done well. My airplane was among the top ten that were pulled into the hangar and inspected to make sure they had not been modified in any way. The standings would not be made public until the debriefing meeting two days later. The debriefing meeting is always a closed meeting for racers and board members only. In case there are any noisy gripes, we like to keep it among ourselves. If someone feels that another racer has done something illegal, she can pay a hundred dollars, file a complaint, and have that person investigated, which is what had happened to me in 1957 on my first race. It was not until the debriefing meeting that I learned that I had won the race with an average speed of more than thirty-four miles per hour over my handicap of one hundred eighteen.

The banquet that night was a wonderful time of celebration for me. Marv and Lois Berger, with whom I share an airplane, flew down and brought Morris and my son, Mike. When someone asked if Morris had brought me flowers, I joked, "He'd better not spend money on flowers. I'd rather he bought gas." In fact, in my earlier days of racing, he did send me flowers, but many times I did not receive them. I do get flowers, however, The first-time racers, for whom I give a seminar at the Illinois race, always get me a rose. They do it every year, yet I am always flattered. At first it was because they were my "chicks," but now it's because we are friends. The trademark Tiger Lily I received from Bonnie and Shirley, who had placed second in their Grumman Tiger, was especially meaningful to me.

Lest people be impressed by the five-thousand-dollar first prize, I will point out that the entry fees, fuel and living expenses for the race can easily add up to half that amount. There's no denying; racing is an expensive hobby. I finally got to put the stones in my Classic pendant; I have twenty now. But I chose something a little less expensive than diamonds. I'd rather buy gas.

> *"When I saw you pass us out of Salinas like we were standing still, I knew you were on your way."*
> —Note from Rita Buhl, fellow racer

North to Alaska

In 1986, the international convention for the Ninety-Nines was in Anchorage, Alaska. The Air Race Classic was just over, and four of us started talking about flying up to the convention. Marion Jayne, who had recently flown around the world, offered to furnish the plane, a twin-engine Piper Commanche, if the rest of us would split the cost of fuel. The price was right. Marion had a condo hangar at the Landings Airport on the west side of Chicago. There was a fellow there who had a light twin-engine Cougar and he started "making noises" that he wanted to go to Alaska too. "If you're going to do it," he said, " could some of us go too?" Marion knew him and knew that he had an instrument ticket. She also knew he had never used it.

She told him, "We are going to Alaska. If we get up there and run into bad weather and you can't fly through it, we're going to leave you behind. Either that, or you can let Margaret fly you through it, and one of your guys can come up and ride with us for awhile." I had Carl Nahrwold fly me up to Chicago to meet the rest of them. The men were there all ready to go. We were still loading up so we told them to go on ahead. "We'll meet you in Sioux Falls," we said. Even though their airplane was faster than ours, we were reasonably sure we could make better time and, sure enough, when we landed in Sioux Falls, they weren't there.

Marion said, "I'm sorry, but we're not waiting for them. If they aren't here by the time we're ready to leave, we're going without them." Still we worried about where they might be. We got something to eat from a vending machine, gassed up the plane and were just walking out, when they walked in. "Where have you guys been?" Marion asked.

"There were some rain showers back there and we had to go around."

"Well, we're gassed up and ready to go. Do you want Margaret to ride with you for awhile?"

"No, we're fine," one replied. I don't think they were ready to admit that they might need a woman to fly them through the weather.

"We're going to Great Falls," Marion told them. "We're going to stay the night, so you can meet us there."

"Why don't we just go on to Calgary?" they asked. "It's just a little farther."

"We're in no hurry," she replied.

When we got to Great Falls, there was no sign of the men, so we checked into a hotel and got cleaned up. Even though the four of us shared one bathroom, we still made it all the way to the dining room before they walked in.

They were up and waiting at the airport the next morning, afraid, I think, that we would leave them behind. We went on up to Calgary and there we decided to fly up through Banff National Park. Located in the Rocky Mountains, it was famous for the spectacular scenery. There would be glaciers and hot springs and we wanted to fly over Lake Louise. The men hesitated. "Maybe Margaret would like to fly our plane now, just to get a feel for it in case she has to fly it later in bad weather," one suggested. We suspected he didn't want to fly it in the mountains, but he wasn't going to admit it. I went back and flew their Cougar and then switched back with my friends at the next stop.

Then we met another friend, Velda King Mapelli, on her way to the convention. "Why don't you fly with me, Margaret? All he wants to do is sit and read," she said, pointing to her passenger, who was her son-in-law. It was a little crowded in the Commanche so I changed planes and flew a leg with her. Then, going through the Northwest Passage, I had to go back and fly the Cougar for the men again due to bad weather. While we were in Anchorage, the four of us women decided to go up to Denali Park. We were flying up and down the glaciers and having a lot of fun, when suddenly it didn't look like Denali Park down there anymore. Finally, we spotted a landing strip and some people so we landed. We taxied up and spoke to the first person we saw. "Could you tell us how far it is to the nearest restaurant?"

He started laughing. "Oh, a hundred, maybe two hundred miles." He explained that a few weeks earlier a plane had disappeared and he was among a search party out looking. The Salvation Army had provided food for the searchers and he invited us to join them. So, before we headed back up to Denali Park, we sat on the side of the landing strip and feasted on hot dogs and soup. All in all, our Alaskan adventure was great fun. We even got the men there safely. Maybe their pride wasn't intact, but their plane was.

ANOTHER VOICE:

Patricia Jayne Keefer
(FRIEND AND FELLOW RACER)

Margaret and I have been racing with and against each other since the late 1960s when my mom, Marion Jayne, formed the first race open to both men and women. Sharing rich memories of races and places and the freedom of flight, we consider Margaret as much a part of our extended family as she is a competitor.

Margaret has never avoided doing the hard things. When Mom became ill with terminal cancer, Margaret called and asked what she could do to help. Mom said, "Just send a funny card."

Margaret, of course, sent a funny card, but also shared her thoughts by writing, "Thank you for inviting me on the 1992 world race... and thank you for believing I could lose 50 pounds to do it. Thank you for pushing me to fly the 1994 world race. Thank you. Thank you. Thank you."

After Mom died, Margaret fell ill and was unable to attend the Chicago memorial service. Wanting to say goodbye to a long-time flying friend and needing the closure of the service, she called another race buddy, Jerry Conners, with an unusual request. Since Jerry was conducting the service, she wanted him to arrange for a videotape of the service. At first it seemed an odd request, but I'm so thankful she did it because now it is a wonderful keepsake. Many attendees stood and shared "Marion Moments," and thanks to Margaret we have some more fun personal remembrances of Mom. As I said, Margaret doesn't avoid doing the hard things that come with life.

Following my mother's death I inherited the presidency of the Marion Jayne U.S. Air Race, the largest cross country race in the world. In March 1997, I needed to fly to six states to attend meetings in eight different cities — 3600 miles in four days — to prepare the route for the race. The only problem was, I couldn't count on the weather being VFR (Visual Flight Rules) when I needed it to be. Not having gotten around to obtaining my instrument license, I needed a friend with an instrument instructor's license to ride along, someone who would be comfortable flying with me at the controls of the Twin Commanche. My first thought was of Margaret, and of course, she agreed. What a team! While I was conducting the meetings, she would check the weather and file the flight plan. Then I would fly. Everywhere we went I'd introduce her as the WASP pilot who had been flying 55 years and tell everyone she would fly anything with wings. We had a great time during the 20 hours of flying and spent almost every other waking moment "hangar flying." Even though it had been almost three years since I had seen Margaret and months since we had talked, it just didn't matter. We were able to pick up right where we left off. Our friendship has endured across distance and time, I believe, because of the many wonderful experiences we have shared at the various cross-country races.

(Top) A stop at Fort Wayne's Baer Field during the 1958 Powder Puff. My copilot (standing on the ground) was my sister-in-law Lois Laymon. (Bottom) With Olive Ann Beech, the owner of Beechcraft. I crossed the finish line first in the plane she provided, but I didn't win.

Our welcome committee following the 1958 Powder Puff. (From the left) My mother, father, and Marsha look on while Mike in the foreground holding Morris's hand seems more interested in the camera than Mom's return.

Copilot Lois Laymon racing to the time clock in the 1959 Powder Puff. We beat the offical sundown by two minutes!

Lois Laymon and me with our "Yellow-tired Champ" in the 1960 Powder Puff.

Leaving Fort Wayne for the 1960 S.M.A.L.L. race in the same little Champion -- minus the yellow tires.

Accepting the first place trophy in the 1960 S.M.A.L.L. race. I wore a plain black dress because I KNEW I wouldn't win.

I crossed the finish line in this Beechcraft in the 1963 Powder Puff Derby.

Marsha and Mom made quite a team in the 1965 Powder Puff Derby

Boarding the Mooney, headed for the start of the 1969 Powder Puff. Copilot Evelyn Bowyer looking on. Note the high heels!

Off to the 1969 Powder Puff.

In Indianapolis with copilot Trudy Cooper preparing for the 1971 Powder Puff Derby.

I won first place in gas consumption in the 1975 Powder Puff and fifth overall in a field of 200. The 1974 race had been cancelled due to a national gas shortage.

Ready to fly the 1978 Air Race Classic solo.

I flew the Air Race Classic solo again in 1988 -- Just me and the Cherokee. Only this time I WON!

PART FIVE

Flying For Hire

"I'm everyone's bad-weather friend."
--Margaret Ringenberg

✈

Adventure in Old Mexico

When Al Jeffers, an attorney from Fort Wayne, approached me with a request to fly him and some friends into Mexico for a dove-hunting expedition, I didn't want to do it at first. For one thing, there aren't many maps of the country, and I had heard horror stories about airplanes left at Mexican airports being stripped. I would be flying the firm's older model Beechcraft Bonanza. The four place plane with a speed of about 190 miles per hour was considered by some to be the Cadillac of airplanes. I loved everything about that plane from its red and white exterior to the arrangement of the instrument panel, and I didn't want to take any chances with it. Finally, I agreed to take them into Mexico if I could take the airplane back to Texas, and then catch a commercial flight home. When they were ready, I would go back to Texas to get the plane and fly them out.

I normally don't waste my energy worrying, but when the men started loading their guns into the plane, I started feeling uncomfortable. They had permits to take them into Mexico and it was a hunting expedition, but there was just something unnerving about flying weapons into a foreign country. We hit our first snag when we crossed the border. I had trouble understanding the tower operator's directions. It flustered me to feel so unsure of myself on the landing. When they summoned me to the tower, I hurried off without the necessary insurance papers and had to make a second trip to the plane. I was already wilting in the heat. Just as I'd expected, there were no current maps of our destination. By flying low enough to follow landmarks, we found the airstrip — a nice modern facility with one blacktop runway and no buildings anywhere, just weeds. There was one other plane parked there and two uniformed policemen who were no more than boys. I didn't want to shut down the engine because then I would have to let it cool down before I could start it again. It was HOT and I wasn't interested in being stuck there for any length of time. The men got out with their gear. "I'll call my wife," Al shouted over the engine noise. "She'll get in touch with you and let you know when to come back." They piled into a pickup truck with a guide and left.

I took the plane back to Harlingen, Texas, as planned and caught an airline home. Back in Fort Wayne, Morris and I went to a pancake breakfast given by the Shriners, where I was presented with an award for my contributions to aviation. I kept expecting to hear from Mrs. Jeffers at any time. When she hadn't called by Sunday, I called her. Surprisingly, she hadn't heard a word from Al, and in fact, had not even known if they got to Mexico all right. I assured her that I had gotten them there safely and that I had come home. Now, I told her, I was planning the trip back to get them.

Trusting my intuition, I decided to head back to Texas, even though they hadn't called. Al had mentioned that he needed to be back by Thursday to prepare a court case. He had gotten me a seat on the airline for Monday afternoon, but I went to the airport hoping to get an earlier flight. The trip back, by way of Chicago, was slowed by bad weather and fog in Houston. When I arrived in Harlingen, I began to worry about the possibility of getting fogged in the next morning at the Fixed Base Operator (FBO). I bought all the pop in the machine and several candy bars, stuffed them into a plastic trash bag, and put it in my suitcase. If I went ahead to the Mexican airstrip and had to spend the night in the plane, I was concerned about the heat and the possibility of dehydration.

The airstrip was deserted, but almost as soon as I taxied in, I saw two armed men come out of the bushes. What, I wondered, had I gotten myself into? Nevertheless, I decided to stay put. They approached the plane, speaking rapid Spanish, which I didn't understand. I answered in English, which they didn't understand. I tried sign language, but how does one make the sign for, "I'm here to pick up three men and I don't have a clue as to where they are?" The guards started laughing. One of them took out a piece of paper and walked around the plane. He compared something on the paper to the number on the plane. He looked at his partner and they burst out laughing again. I wasn't amused.

Still laughing, they handed me the paper. It was from Al. "Couldn't find a phone," it said. I learned later that Al had paid the two guards to watch for the plane and deliver a note to the pilot. He had neglected to tell them that the pilot would be a sixty-seven-year-old grandmother. I forget sometimes that even now, women pilots are not a common sight in some countries. Al wanted me to meet his party at a lodge about a mile west of town. What he had overlooked was how I was supposed to get there. My two companions couldn't read the note, and so far my sign language had been less than effective. The sun was so hot, I climbed down and walked around to sit in the shade of the airplane. One of the men went running off down a path. The other one was so nervous, he kept his hand on his gun the whole time. I was more amused than frightened. Did he think I was going to make a run for it?

After awhile, the first man came back with another Mexican, driving an old, beat-up car, and motioned that I was to go with him. Warning bells went off in my head about strangers and cars, but what was my alternative? Sit out in the sun and die of heatstroke? I noticed a dirty card above the visor that appeared to be some sort of official document. I convinced myself that he was a legitimate cab driver, but since I didn't read Spanish, it could have been a fishing license, for all I know. We had gone barely a hundred feet when a tire blew. What next? The driver went around and looked at the tire, then unwired the glove compartment, took out a key and went around to the trunk. He motioned that I should stay in the car. I looked down and shook my head in disbelief. After all the business with the armed guard, this guy got out of the car, leaving his gun on the seat beside me. Either he had decided I wasn't a threat or he wasn't very bright. He was back there so long, I started to get out of the car to see what was going on. He quickly motioned me back into the car. I never did find out what was in the trunk, but obviously it wasn't a spare tire. He got back in and we limped into town on the rim.

Finally, I spotted three young people I thought might be from the United States. I asked. They were Canadian. Close enough. "Do you know where this lodge is?" I asked, showing them the note. They didn't, so they turned to ask a man sitting in a pickup truck. He didn't know either, but the little boy with him did and they offered me a ride. When we pulled up to a house, there was no sign or anything to indicate it was a lodge. My driver left me and I found myself alone with a woman who spoke no English. She tried sign language and this time I understood the gesture when she pointed at me and laid her head on her hands. Yes, I was tired. She showed me to a little room. I had no intention of sleeping; I just wanted to get away from her and the way she watched my every move. In my room, I discovered that my pop cans had sweat all over everything in the suitcase, so I was busy spreading things out to dry when I heard a man's voice downstairs. I ran down, thinking it was Al and the others. It wasn't't.

It was then that I noticed that the table was set for eight people. Maybe that was an indication that I was in a lodge, although whether or not it was the right lodge, I didn't know. My hostess made eating motions. I nodded. Yes, I was hungry. At least I was until I smelled the meat she was cooking. When she brought me a plate with a large thin steak on it, I had no idea if it was for me or for everyone. I cut off a small piece and gave it back. There was avocado, (that seemed safe) and a bowl of what I thought was green applesauce. I took a big spoon full. Instantly I realized my mistake. It was not applesauce, but jalapeno relish! My mouth was on fire. I cried out the only English word I thought she might know: "Coca Cola!" She understood.

When Al and the others finally showed up, Al was so glad to see me he threw his arms around me and hugged me. I tried not to let on that the feeling was mutual. I learned that they had not been able to find a working phone to call home so they had not known if or when I would show up. They had been quite worried, but now that I was there, they were not ready to go home. They just had to get in one more morning of hunting. It would be too foggy to fly out before the next afternoon anyway, they rationalized. Right then and there, I decided to take up dove hunting. I was not going to spend another day with that woman staring at me, especially when our common vocabulary consisted of two words.

After we got back to Fort Wayne, Al invited Morris and me to the Country Club for a wild game feast that included the Mexican white doves. We had a great time, until each of the men got up and started telling about the trip. I was worried that Morris would be upset when he heard the details of my adventure, but he seemed to take it all in stride. I guess he's used to it by now. Besides, it got us an invitation to the Country Club, and that doesn't happen every day.

ANOTHER VOICE:

Tony Niewyk

Flying back from Washington DC in the Bonanza one time, Margaret spotted storm clouds ahead. She got on the horn. "Can you vector us around them? she asked the controller. When he thought we were past the storm, he got us back on course. Unfortunately, we still caught the edge of the storm. All of a sudden the plane started dropping at about 1,000 feet a minute. We shot straight up, in spite of the seatbelts and banged our heads on the ceiling. It was quite a shock. I was struggling to tighten my seatbelt and talk to the controller.

"Man, you guys are going all over the place," he told us. But Margaret was perfectly in charge. She never got rattled.. Another time coming back from DC our alternator went out. We turned off the radio to conserve power. Continuing to fly by VFR (Visual Flight Rules), Margaret landed us safely at Smith Field using the radio at the last moment when necessary. She knew what to do and how to do it.

✈

The Honky-tonk Blues

There is a real mix of people, airplanes, weather, and hotels involved when I work as a pilot "for hire." I'm reminded of a trip I had to Cookville, Tennessee, with three salesmen. Because they had not wanted to pay extra for a twin-engine airplane, I was flying a more economical Cherokee 180 with fixed gear and fixed prop. Looking back, I wonder how I happened to procure the trip. I suspect it was because everyone else was busy and no one else wanted it. At the time, I was just glad to have the trip. We had a good trip and the men rented a car and dropped me at a little "mom and pop" motel. The only phone was in the office, and the snack machine out front was the closest thing they had to a restaurant.

Looking around, I decided I was lucky to have that. The television had little to offer in the way of entertainment so I planned to settle in with a good book. About 6 p.m., the men came to my door to tell me there was a dinner at the American Legion and we were going.

"Thanks, but I already had something from the snack machine," I told them. They insisted. In fact they would not take "no" for an answer. This particular county in Tennessee was "dry," meaning there was no liquor legally sold there, but it was obvious that my companions had been drinking somewhere before they picked me up. I soon found out that the Legion wasn't "dry" either. The dinner was good homestyle food, but I was anxious to get back to the motel and my book. When someone told them about a nearby honky-tonk, they were off to find it with me in tow. I was extremely uncomfortable when I found out a password was required to enter the club in the back room of the establishment. I felt as though I was in an old Prohibition movie. As soon as we were in and seated at a table, I excused myself to go to the restroom. I searched in vain for a pay phone. Finally I asked the clerk if there were any cabs in the area.

"Yes," he said, MUCH to my relief.

"Would you call one for me? And please don't tell anyone." I went outside to wait. Before long, I saw one of the men come out and look around. I hid behind some bushes and prayed that the cab wouldn't arrive while he was standing there. Finally, he went back inside and after a considerable wait, the cab came and took me back to the motel. I didn't sleep well, and several hours later

I heard loud talking as the men returned. The next morning when it got close to our agreed-upon time to leave, I opened my door and set my suitcase outside. When I heard them coming, I stepped out and greeted them. "Good morning," I said, thinking quickly of an excuse I could make about last night if anyone asked. No one did. We loaded our things in the car, stopped at a diner for breakfast and went back to the plane. We had a good flight home, and not once did anyone mention the previous evening. I guess I should have been relieved, but I was a little miffed. I had "disappeared" from a honky-tonk bar late at night in a strange town, and not one of my companions even noticed!

ANOTHER VOICE:

G. Michael Livingston

When I started flying, Margaret would often call and ask me to ride along with her whenever she had a trip alone. It wasn't that she needed a copilot, she just liked having someone along to talk to. Even though she can give the impression that she is a quiet person, when she gets to know someone well she will talk and talk especially if the subject is airplanes. She just can't hide her passion for flying.

She called me to ride along with her one night in August 1980 when she was hired to deliver a deposition to the courthouse in Parkersburg, West Virginia. Because she had to have it there by eight a.m. the next day, we left Fort Wayne in the wee hours of the morning. About midway to

Parkersburg, everything electrical in the cockpit of the Piper Cherokee went dead. Of course, since the engine ran on magnetos rather than electricity, we were not in danger of losing power, but it was very dark in the cockpit! Margaret remained calm. It was comforting to me that she did not consider it an emergency situation. We found a flashlight and I replaced the fuses without success. Margaret just kept flying. "How are we going to get the plane started again," I asked, "once we turn it off?"

"We'll just get a jump start," she answered. She wasn't the least bit flustered, and I remember how much my confidence in her ability grew that day. Looking back, I realize that it wasn't just her cool head that kept her going that day, it was the fact that she had made a commitment. People were counting on her and she was determined not to let them down.

Another time we had planned to fly my father to Massillon, Ohio, for a business appointment. In order to get him there in time for his meeting, we had allowed ourselves an hour and a half for the flight. Margaret, however, was overdue returning from another flight and as the minutes ticked away, my father gave up hope of getting to Massillon on time. With just an hour remaining, Margaret taxied up and got out of the plane. "Are you ready?" she asked. "Let's go." My father was nervous and frustrated, but Margaret seemed to have things under control. There were thunderstorms in the area, but believe it or not, Margaret actually liked to fly in thunderstorms because she knew how to use the counter-clockwise winds to her advantage. Forty-five minutes later, thanks to great tailwinds, we arrived in Massillon with time to spare!

Sometimes I flew with Margaret when she had corporate passengers or when she was instructing other students. Whether her customer was a congressman, an architect, or a lawyer, it made no difference to her. She was not intimidated by men or position. Often she would have to correct what she considered bad habits that her students had acquired before coming to her. She wanted them to do it her way. Many of these were professional men and, I feel sure, not accustomed to taking orders from anyone, especially a woman. But, when Margaret told them what to do, they did it without question. Still there have been times, I know, when she has not been given the respect she deserves simply because she is a woman.

Once when we flew together up to London, Ontario, Canada, we were sitting in the plane on the ground, waiting for customs' officials to come and clear us. We had been sitting there for at least a half hour and no one came, so we called the tower and asked for permission to get out of the airplane in order to place a telephone call to customs. As soon as we got out, another pilot saw us and warned us that getting out of the airplane before being cleared by customs was an illegal act subject to fine.

We were waiting in the plane when the customs' officer showed up a few minutes later. He was furious, having seen us get out and back into the plane. Ordering us out of the plane, he threatened us with a five-hundred-dollar fine. Margaret stepped up to explain that we had been given permission by tower personnel when the officer cut her off in mid-sentence and turned to me. Totally ignoring her, he began to ask me questions. Apparently it had not occurred to him that Margaret might be the pilot. In his mind, I was the pilot because I was a man.

I was quite aggravated, but Margaret handled it with poise, never refuting his assumption or offering proof that she indeed was the pilot-in-command. She just stepped back and let me answer the questions. Afterward her only comment was, "Now wasn't that interesting?" I believe, in the face of such bias, she simply finds it unnecessary to defend herself. She lets her ability speak for her.

Margaret is my hero and over the years I have described her to other people as a modern-day Amelia Earhart. I know she shies away from such a comparison, but I truly do look at her that way and, in my opinion, her accomplishments have certainly earned her that designation.

Morris Ringenberg

Congressman Dan Coats and I had offices together at one time. We saw each other daily so whenever he needed to go someplace in a hurry, I would volunteer Margaret. I imagine it was through Dan Coats or someone else connected with the Republican Headquarters that she came to fly Dan Quayle when he was running for the Senate. She has flown several of our governors as well as a few politicians who didn't get elected, but we don't talk about them.

✈

All Work and No Play?
Hardly!

Flying for hire has its "perks" too. Once I deliver my passengers, my time is my own until it's time for the return trip. When I have to stay overnight, it is wonderful to take a long bath, relax and read without the phone ringing. Once on a trip to Greenville, South Carolina, I left a message for Carolyn Pilaar, who was a pilot for Pan Am. I thought she might call, but a knock on the door caught me by surprise. Staying alone in a motel, I confess, sometimes makes me more nervous than the trip to Mexico. Anyway, Carolyn and I enjoyed a nice visit, and then she invited me and Gary Ann Wheeler, a fellow air racer, to visit her in Berlin, Germany, on a companion pass. When we went, we got to stay on military bases because I had a military pass, but the highlight of the trip was getting my own piece of the Berlin Wall. Did I say I don't scare easily? That was before I was introduced to the Autobahn. Now that's scary!

While solitude can be nice at times, there are some places I don't enjoy going alone. One of them is Florida. What fun is it to swim and lie on the beach by yourself? That's where grandkids come in. So when Max Miller, a local architect, asked me to fly him to Florida on business, I thought of Jaala. My five-year-old granddaughter loved to fly, and Marsha agreed it would be all right to take her out of nursery school for a few days. It would be a special treat for her to escape the cold Indiana weather.

Max had several projects going in several other states as well as Florida, so we were going by way of Milwaukee, where he was to meet with a building inspector. Within a few hours we planned to be on our way to the warm, sunny beaches of Florida. Whenever I have my grandchildren along, I try to check in on a daily basis to assure their parents they are all right. I called Marsha that night. "Guess where we are?"

"Florida," she said.

"No, Milwaukee."

" You're still in Milwaukee?" she asked. "What happened?"

"The inspector didn't show up so we have to wait until tomorrow," I told her. Marsha wondered about Jaala being warm enough, since she had filled her suitcase with shorts and swimsuits. After all, it was only about 5 degreees in Milwaukee. I promised she was warm enough in the winter clothes she had been wearing when we left home. They would last another day.

The next night I called Marsha again. "Guess where we are?"

"Not Milwaukee, I hope."

"No. We're in sunny Florida." I bragged about the warm weather and put Jaala on the phone. "Tell your mom what you've been doing," I prompted.

"We went to McDonald's and there was a palm tree in front," she squealed.

The next night I called again. "Guess where we are?" I was enjoying this game.

"Florida."

"No, San Antonio."

"Texas? What are you doing there?" Marsha wanted to know. I explained that Max had gotten a call to go and check on some work in Texas. On the way we had stopped in New Orleans.

"Here's Jaala," I said, handing her the phone. When I took the phone back, Marsha was laughing. "What's so funny," I asked.

"I asked Jaala what she had seen on all her travels."

"What did she say?"

"The inside of five clouds!"

Weather can sometimes add a little interest to what should be a routine trip. I had flown Chuck Chafee and some other men from the Bluffton Rubber Company to Detroit on business. Following his meeting they needed to get right back to Indiana for an early morning appointment the next day. But when they returned to the airport in Detroit following their meeting, I had to inform them we were fogged in. "Then we'll just take the airline home," Chuck decided. I didn't say a word. He came back a few minutes later. "The airlines can't fly out either," he grumped. Surprise.

His next idea was to rent a car. "If you just wait a little while, " I told them, "when the cooler air rolls in, the fog should lift."

But they couldn't wait, so they rented a car and started out in a pea soup fog for Fort Wayne. I sat awhile at the FBO until the benches got too hard, and then I went to the airplane and slept quite comfortably the rest of the night. As I had expected, the next morning the sky was clear. I filed my flight plan and headed for Indiana, arriving at the airport just ahead of my customers. I wisely kept my comments to myself.

ANOTHER VOICE:

G. Michael Livingston

One trait I admire about Margaret is her generosity. Without hesitation she would let me borrow her airplane or lend me her brand new GPS (Global Positioning System). She has always been willing to help and be available whenever someone needs her. On one occasion we were out at Fort Wayne Air Service when we overheard a man discussing his need to get to Chicago for a meeting. He had a Piper Navajo, but he was worried about flying it himself. Chicago was such a busy area that the prospect of dealing with Air Traffic Control was obviously intimidating to him. Seeing how agitated he was, Margaret walked over to him and said, "I'll take you." It wasn't the first time she had offered to become the security blanket for another pilot who was uncertain or uncomfortable with certain flying conditions. So, even though we had just returned from a trip, we climbed into his plane and flew him to Chicago.

Later when we got ready to leave Chicago Midway, Margaret was given some very short parameters in which to take off. She handled the pressure of taking off in busy traffic in a complicated airplane while I handled the radio. We made a good team.

Anytime a person called Margaret for help, she could be ready to jump into the car within fifteen minutes and head for the airport. On the night of June 18, 1989, when my wife's father who lived in Pikeville, Kentucky, suffered a heart attack, I was the one who called her. I had agreed to fly my wife and her sisters to Kentucky, but I was feeling a little uncomfortable about doing it alone on such short notice. It was nine o'clock when I called Margaret, asking her to ride with me. By ten o'clock we were at the airport ready to taxi out. Suddenly everything in the cockpit went black. This time it was Margaret who was uncomfortable with the idea of taking off with only a flashlight to illuminate the instrument panel. "I need to do this," I said. Let's at least try it and if it doesn't work, we can turn around and come back." She agreed and we made the flight without incident. Afterward she confessed that she would not have attempted that by herself. I remember being impressed that, with all her experience, she was humble enough to admit to me, her student, that she had moments of doubt, too. Through her example that night, I learned to maintain a healthy respect for flying no matter what my level of expertise.

Morris Ringenberg

People are always asking me, "Don't you worry about Margaret when she flies?"I tell them, "Not anymore than when she is driving to the airport." If I was one to worry, I would be worried all the time since she is always either in a car or a plane. When she flew around the world, I had not studied the routes ahead of time. I didn't really know exactly when and where she was flying over the water or where she was at any given time until she called me. If I haven't worried about her in the more than fifty years we have been married, I guess I won't start now. Mike and I did fine "holding down the fort" at home, and I think the local restaurants approved of her trip.

Since the world race she has become a celebrity of sorts and people are always asking me, "Where is Margaret today?" Not long ago I was in New York on business and I overheard Margaret's name. I just listened as they discussed my wife and how they had seen her at the airport and how impressed they were with the number of flying hours she has. Recently I drove her and my daughter to Indianapolis just before she was to catch a flight to Colorado to speak at the Air Force Academy. A man approached me in the lobby of the hotel and said, "I think I've seen you someplace and I think you are Margaret Ringenberg's husband."

Having a wife who is a pilot has its advan-

tages, too. One time I was playing in a golf tournament in Florida and I was scheduled to tee off at
one o'clock on a Saturday afternoon. A snowstorm
in Fort Wayne delayed our takeoff until the runways could be cleared. It seemed unlikely that we
could get there in time. In this particular Florida
town, however, many people had hangars instead
of garages. Cars and airplanes shared the streets
and airplanes had the right-of-way. Margaret
landed the plane close to the golf course where
my partner was waiting with a golf cart. We transferred the clubs from the plane to the cart, raced
off to the golf course, and arrived to tee off right
on time.

*"Sometimes it is amazing to me how many things in my
life have just come together. I have always believed it must
be God's leading. That may be the reason why even during
experiences like Mexico I'm not especially afraid. I like the
adventure. I couldn't wait to get home and tell the story."*
--Margaret Ringenberg

PART SIX

Flying Around the World

"It is quite likely. . .that her more adventurous days may be over, for young, gray-eyed Mrs. Ringenberg . . . finds herself under the restraining influence of a husband and a two-year-old daughter."—Excerpt from The (Fort Wayne) *News Sentinel*, December 9, 1949

245

✈

Opportunity Knocks
1993

This is Philip Reames," the voice at the other end of the line said when I answered the phone.

"Yes?" I stalled as my mind clicked through all the Reameses I knew in the area. I couldn't place him.

"From California," he added, as if that would explain everything. "Doctor Philip Reames from California. I'm planning to fly in a race around the world next year, and I'm looking for a competent pilot to go with me. I'm told you're one of the best." I was speechless for a moment.

As soon as I recovered from the surprise, I corrected him. "I wouldn't consider myself a competent pilot for a race like that." Even though I had been racing for 36 years and had close to 40,000 hours of flying time, I had never filed a flight plan over water. Furthermore, I had never even heard of some of the places he was telling me about.

"I would pick up all of the cost," he added, "except your room and board." Maybe that seemed like a minor detail to him, but, as events were to prove, my share would be around thirteen thousand dollars! "I'm looking for a pilot, not a girlfriend," he assured me, as if that had even occurred to me. My husband of forty-eight years would be glad to know, I'm sure, that if I were to fly around the world, it would be strictly business. Of course, I wasn't going to fly around the world, so it didn't matter. "Well, think about it," he said. "If you're not interested, maybe you know someone else in your racing circles who can help me out. I really want to beat Marion Jayne." At that I could only laugh. Marion, who had beat me in the Air Race Classic more than once, was a tough competitor. I told him I would like to beat Marion too, but I knew what kind of plane she had. After I hung up, I tried to call Morris. When I couldn't get through, I tried Marsha. No answer. Mike was at work, so I was nearly bursting with the news when Morris got home.

"Of course I'm not thinking of doing it," I said. "It would cost too much and I would have to be gone for thirty days." I thought of other reasons — I wanted, for instance, to attend the Women in Aviation Conference in March and that would take money. There was the Air Race Classic coming up in June. I couldn't miss that. The twenty-fifth anniversary of the Illinois race was coming up, and I was to be honored for flying every one of them. I wanted to be there. But when Morris started naming other pilots he had heard me mention, I systematically eliminated each one for various reasons.

The next morning, Carolyn Pilaar came to mind. She had been a pilot for Pan Am, had experience flying overseas, and she was a mechanic. She would be perfect for this race. I dialed her number. "Oh, Margaret!" she said, and I knew right away she wanted to do it. "But I just got hired on with a carrier and I start training next week. I can't ask for the entire month of May off when I just got the job. You have to do it."

After I hung up, my mind was whirling. "You have to do it," Carolyn had said. I wanted to, but there were a dozen reasons why I couldn't. Even so, when I was at the airport, I couldn't resist walking through the hangars looking for a Cessna 414, the kind of plane Doc Reames had mentioned in his call. The 414, with a nice roomy cabin, could be entered by walking in from the back, but it was not air-conditioned or pressurized. "What's the range on the 414? What speeds can it get?" I asked anyone who might know. I wasn't going; I was just curious.

The next week, on the way into town with my daughter, I started recounting my conversation with Carolyn. "What are you talking about?" Marsha asked. Suddenly I realized I had been talking the whole thing over with myself so much I had completely forgotten to tell her. "You're going to do it, aren't you, Mom?" she said. "It's such a great opportunity."

"Well, he said he would send me a packet of

GIRLS CAN'T BE PILOTS

information and that was a week ago." I replied.
"Maybe he found someone else." I was surprised
at how disappointed I felt, even though I was going to turn him down.

Then on September 28 the packet arrived
with the information and race route. I had to get
the atlas to find some of the places and wondered
how I would get maps. I called Marion Jayne. "You
should do it," she told me. But when I brought up
the cost issue, she said, "You wouldn't be able to
room with us. The rooms are too small for a roll-
away bed. I guess if you get in a bind you could
bunk on the floor. Do fly the race, Margaret." I
questioned her about the maps and she told me
she used the ONC charts. I thanked her and hung
up, thinking that now all I had to do was find out
what an ONC chart was. I asked everyone I knew.
It was small comfort that none of them knew either. Finally I talked to an airline pilot who directed me to a catalog where I could order them. I
tried to plot out the race course on the tiny pictures in the catalog and figure out what number I
needed to order. I made a few costly mistakes before I got the ones I needed. Sprawled out on the
floor, struggling to read the small print, holding
the maps down and drawing the lines at the same
time, I was about ready to give it all up, when
Joanne, the young Amish woman who helps me
around the house, came to the rescue. Between
the two of us, we got the lines drawn, but I'm sure
we made quite a sight.

"You're not thinking of doing it, are you?"
my sister-in-law asked.

"Gee, I guess I am," I admitted for the first
time. When another family friend accused me of

trying to be another Amelia Earhart, I disagreed. "I'm much too old for that," I said, even though I didn't feel old. I began to consider what other people would think about a grandmother of five flying around the world. Funny how I had never worried about that before. Not long after that, I went with Morris to a bank board meeting in Indianapolis. While the board was meeting, I went shopping with some of the wives. Sitting around a table in the lobby later, I decided to test the waters. "What would you think if I told you I was considering flying around the world with a doctor from California? He'll pay most of the expenses."

They barely let me finish. "What an opportunity! You're going to do it, aren't you?" Several of them told me I'd be crazy not to do it, although they admitted they wouldn't even fly across the state with me in a small plane. I told myself it was a reflection on the plane, not my flying ability. From that point on, I guess I knew I was going. I didn't know how, but I was going.

For the next few weeks, I was busy trying to keep up with my corporate flying, take care of my house, plan for the race and study charts. Then, in the midst of all the activity, Morris's father passed away. I couldn't help but think of the irony. Morris's mother had died during my first race back in 1957. Was it a sign?

The following Sunday, after the funeral, Doc Reames called. "I got the plane, but I decided on a 340 instead of the 414," he said. "The aisles are narrow, but the cabin is air-conditioned and pressurized." He was seventy-six and I was seventy-three, so it would be easier on us if we didn't have to use oxygen. Even so, I questioned the decision.

I didn't think we stood a chance of winning with the 340. It was handicapped too high. The manufacturers, proud of their little plane, had projected that it would go faster than it actually did. In a handicapped race, their optimism would be a real detriment, costing us points on every leg. It would be an accomplishment just to finish, but I at least wanted a fair shot at winning. Still, I kept my opinions to myself. It was his race. "I have to go to Australia to pick it up," Doc continued. "I don't want to fly back alone. Will you go?" I didn't know what to say.

Morris was in Myrtle Beach playing golf so I couldn't discuss it with him. I turned my house upside-down in a fruitless search for my passport. Then I came down with the flu. "I never thought how much was involved in all this," I lamented when my husband returned. "I don't know how to file the flight plan. I don't know how much money to take. I don't know where to buy gas. And now he wants me to go to Australia. I don't know if I can do this."

"Well, you've never been to Australia," he replied. To him it was as simple as that. I thought about my husband's standard remark about our trade-off between his golf and my flying, but in all fairness, he has never circled the globe in search of a golf course. Still there was the problem of the missing passport. It was not in the house. I was certain of that. Morris checked the bank to see if it was in the safe deposit box. It wasn't. Meanwhile, I called Linda Murphy, who is a travel agent, to check on the cost of the flight to California and then to Australia, and she told me what to do about the passport.

252

At the post office, I filled out a lost passport form. When I explained how quickly it was needed, the woman at the desk looked doubtful, but as soon as I filled out the paperwork, she closed down her station and took it upstairs to have the proper individual process it and get it off to Chicago. I called Marion again. "If he wants to hire me, I'll go to Australia and get the plane," she offered. But when I told Doc, he explained that he knew a ferry pilot who would fly with us if I didn't want to go alone. That sounded better to me. I would be able to ride and learn the procedures from someone who was experienced before I had to try it myself. The Pacific Ocean would be an intimidating place for a woman who normally avoids flying over the Great Lakes.

On the seventeenth of November, I called Chicago and they assured me my passport was being processed and would be in the mail shortly. I waited. Saturday passed. Now Monday would be the earliest it could arrive. Then on Sunday Mike came in the house and said, "Oh, I almost forgot. This came for you yesterday." He tossed me the passport. He had gone to pick up the mail, stuck it in his car, and forgotten about it. I immediately called Doc.

"I have the passport, but there's no chance I can get a visa, too, in a week," I told him.

"Just put it in an envelope," he advised, "with a letter saying that you are making me your agent for the purpose of obtaining a visa and 'overnight' it to me." He would try to get the visa, but if not, we could pick it up when I got to California. The next evening he called to say he had the visa and everything was under control.

Linda did her best to get me a ticket to Los Angeles on the twenty-ninth, but due to the Thanksgiving holiday and problems at American Airlines, the best she could do was the thirtieth, the same day we were to leave for Australia. I would be cutting it close. She kept checking, however, and finally she found a flight on the twenty-ninth by way of Cincinnati and Atlanta. Oh well, what's another thousand miles or so?

I arrived at LAX without incident and there was no one to meet me. I had not brought Doc's phone number, knowing it was his office number and I would get the answering machine anyway. I had him paged. When he still didn't come, I called home to get the number and left a message on his machine telling him that I was waiting at Delta Gate 57A. While I was waiting I became engrossed in an announcement made over the airport's loudspeaker offering a free round-trip ticket to anyone willing to give up a seat on the next flight. I guess no one took them up on it because the offer was sweetened to a round trip ticket plus fifty dollars. The next offer was for a hundred dollars, and then two hundred dollars and some sort of certificate. When Doc finally arrived to pick me up, I was almost ready to claim the ticket myself. Really, I hated to leave before I found out how the drama ended.

When opportunity knocks, open the door!
—Margaret Ringenberg

✈

The Land Down Under

★★★★ **Sydney is the largest city in Australia and is sometimes called the "gateway to the continent" because most foreign visitors pass through it. Most of the early inhabitants were convicts sent out from Great Britain, but increasing numbers of free settlers arrived in the 19th century as it was developed by sheep and cattle ranchers and wheat farmers. It has a temperate climate and boasts at least some sunshine 342 days a year. Its population is over 3,000,000.** ★★★★

We left Los Angeles on November 30 and arrived in Sydney on December 2 even though it was only a seventeen-hour flight. My first experience with the International Dateline left me confused for the rest of the trip.

To me, everything in Australia was mixed up. We had just celebrated Thanksgiving at home, but in Australia it was late spring. Then there was the pesky problem about which side of the street to use. Every time I walked out to get into a car or board a bus, I went to the wrong side. I got tired of hearing, "Hey, American, we get in on the correct side here." It was a good thing I wasn't doing the driving because the traffic laws were a bit different too. A driver doesn't have to be pulled over to get a ticket. Running a red light, for example, triggers a camera that takes a picture of the car, and the driver gets a fine in the mail! Even on the highway, cameras register the speed of a car and photograph the license plate. It would make opening the mail an adventure, I guess.

We went into Sydney with the intentions of exchanging our money and having lunch, but when we got there Doc realized that he had left all his cash, a considerable amount, lying on the table in his room. We went back to the hotel to retrieve his money and grab a bite. The salad bar looked good until I found out it cost twenty-five dollars. I settled for a six dollar hamburger instead. As soon as we could, we hailed a ride to Bankstown Airport where the plane was being custom fitted. Doc decided to go across the country to check out another plane so I was on my own for a few days. I enjoyed walking down to the harbor and taking pictures. When Doc returned we went to check on the progress of the plane. It seemed to speed up a bit when he got back. I guess they weren't in a hurry to finish it until they were sure they would be paid.

When our ferry pilot, Peter Cousins, arrived he promptly spotted a problem. Two extra thirty-seven gallon tanks had been installed in the fuselage, leaving about eighteen inches between the tank and the ceiling. We would have to get on our bellies and scoot over the tanks and up to the seats in front, a maneuver neither Doc nor I felt we could manage. Moreover, with three of us in the plane, one of the tanks would have to be removed to make room for an extra seat behind the copilot. Even with Peter flying the plane alone from Hawaii to

California, a distance of 2,500 miles, he would be in a precarious situation, in that one of the extra tanks covered the emergency handle. If he should experience engine failure, he would not be able to get out.

Our luggage and the life boat were stored in the back, but if a serious problem developed and we went down, there was no way we could climb back there to the boat. Behind the copilot's seat was the hatchet and emergency door. The radio hookup and things for the emergency radio and special radio we had to have along were stored under the third seat. Between the two front seats was a radio for high frequency on which we would report all our positions as we went along. I could see that it was going to be cramped quarters.

We moved our gear from Sydney to a motel near Bankstown, expecting to fly out from there. Then we realized the runway was too short for the plane carrying three of us and all the extra fuel. We checked out and went back to Sydney to wait for Peter to pick us up at the larger airport. When he didn't come and didn't come, we called Bankstown. "A little problem with the fuel pump," he said. "They're working on it." Since it was already too late to make Norfolk Island, our first stop, before dark, we checked back into the Sydney Sheraton. I bet the desk clerk thought we were crazy.

The next day, December 8, which, incidentally, was December 7 on my calendar, we took off from the Sydney airport at 11 a.m. It seemed like an awfully long run down the runway before we finally lifted off the ground. Within minutes we were over the shoreline of Australia at 3,000 feet.

It took another twenty minutes to climb to 8,000. Peter explained that he wanted to keep the engine cool, so he was trying not to climb too quickly. It was extremely warm in the cabin, even though we put the enroute chart over the front window to keep the sun out. By afternoon, however, we were picking up ice. It had collected slowly on the leading edge of the wing, but because the plane was white, we hadn't noticed it. We made a note to put black tape on that area before the race so we could see the ice forming and be aware of it sooner. De-icing equipment took care of most of it, but about sixty miles out of Norfolk Island, Peter started the descent to get rid of the ice still under the wings.

One thing I really enjoyed about the trip was experimenting with my new Global Positioning System. I had bought my first GPS about a week before Phil Reames had contacted me, and thinking I would never use it outside the United States, I had bought the GPS 55, which had all the airports and VOR's in North America. I spent hours sitting in the car in my driveway with the GPS plugged into the cigarette lighter before I figured out how to work it. All I had to do was put in the name of the intersection at the latitude and longitude and it would give me the heading for that place. I thought it was pretty simple, but coming into Norfolk Island, I kept getting a misreading. I knew that the heading that showed on my GPS was not the one for Norfolk Island. Peter was not familiar with that particular model so he didn't know what the problem was either. Suddenly it dawned on me that we were not in the Northern Hemisphere. I had not thought about the latitudes and longitudes being S and E now instead of the N and W I was used to. After I got my head in the correct hemisphere, the GPS worked great. The airplane had its own GPS, more costly than my hand-held model, but I felt confident that when the time came I would know how to work it. We landed on Norfolk Island six hours and thirty minutes after leaving Sydney. I was surprised how quickly the time had passed.

✮✮✮✮ **Norfolk Island is a small volcanic island located in the SW Pacific Ocean east of Australia. It was discovered by Captain James Cook and was used by the British as a penal colony in the late 18th and early 19th centuries. Many residents are descendants of HMS Bounty mutineers. It is now an Australian territory and a popular vacation spot for Australians and New Zealanders. Its population numbers about 2,000.** ✮✮✮✮

Customs was waiting for us when we arrived. Norfolk Island was a beautiful place, but we had a terrible time getting something to eat. The first restaurant we tried had a Christmas party going on upstairs, and all the help was working there. Peter remembered another restaurant at the bottom of a steep hill, but after trudging all the way down there, we discovered it was no longer in existence. Doc was unhappy about the prospect of climbing the hill again, so Peter went back up alone to get the van. He took so long that we ended up climbing the hill anyway to see what had happened to him. Finally we found someone to take us to another restaurant, but by that time Peter said he wasn't hungry anymore and went back to his room to do paperwork.

The next day as we were boarding, the bottom step on the plane broke. Consequently, it was at least thirty inches from the ground up to the door. Being six feet tall, Peter could easily step up, but for the rest of the trip, Doc and I needed a boost from behind every time we had to crawl up there. Worse yet, shortly after we left Norfolk Island we noticed gas leaking from one of the auxiliary tanks into the cockpit. Lines from the extra tanks in the fuselage and nose ran up between the left and right seats where the valves were located. By turning the valve on top of the tank in the fuselage, we could equalize the pressure inside and outside of the tank to keep it from collapsing, but since the nose compartment was not pressurized, I wasn't sure why the gas was burbling back into the cockpit. I added it to my list of things to have checked when we got home. The rest of the trip was without incident and we arrived in Samoa nine hours and fifteen minutes later.

★★★★ **Pago Pago pronounced Pango Pango, the capital of American Samoa, is located in an extinct volcano crater on Tutuila Island in the Pacific Ocean. The distribution and tourist center of the island group and a major port and international airport, it experiences frequent and heavy rainfall due to the tropical marine climate. About 3,000 people inhabit the town.** ★★★★

We hired a taxi, which was pretty beat-up by American standards. The driver, dressed in the traditional skirt, said it would cost ten dollars to go to the hotel, which was across a mountain on the other side of the island. The roads were narrow and traffic surprisingly heavy. The hotel was quaint with rattan furniture in the lobby. We asked for a room in the new part, as Peter had instructed. "That is twenty dollars more," the clerk told us, but we weren't taking any chances. Some time back an airplane had rammed into one wing of the hotel, and that section was still in a state of disrepair. I got my key and waited to see what Doc's room number would be. "Whenever you're ready to go eat," I said, "just give me a call." I waited. Finally I tried calling his room, but there was no answer so I went down to the lobby to see if he was there. He wasn't. I found a bell boy, who said, "When your friend got to his room, there was no TV so he didn't want that room." They had moved him to another room with a television, but a non-functional telephone. I had no idea where he was. Then, when Doc finally showed up, Peter had disappeared again. Later, Doc and I were just finishing dinner when Peter showed up without explanation. The dining room was closing so he bought a box of cookies on the way back to the hotel. This man had the most erratic eating habits!

We planned to leave Samoa very early in the morning in order to get to Christmas Island before dark, since there were no lights on the airstrip there. We had breakfast at 6:30, but by the time we drove around the island to get to the plane it was closer to 8:30 when we left. To complicate matters, we were about one hour out of Christmas Island on auto-pilot when both engines quit. First one sputtered and then the other. Since there were no gas gauges on any of the tanks, it was necessary to run on one until it was nearly empty, then switch to another full one. Apparently, when switching, we had switched to another empty tank.

At any rate, it was a tense moment until the right tank was switched on and the engines started up again. If I had been sleepy before, I was certainly awake after that. Sitting in back, I made it a point to keep my eye on the gauges, since at times both Doc and Peter were asleep. We crossed the equator. Coupled with the confusion of the International Dateline, I had absolutely no idea what day it was, let alone the time when we landed on Christmas Island.

★★★★**Christmas Island is the largest atoll in the Pacific of purely coral formation. It was uninhabited when it was discovered in 1777 by Captain James Cook. It was eventually annexed by Great Britain. A U.S. air base during World War II, and now an international air facility, it once served as the site for both U.S. and British nuclear testing. The people, whose chief source of income is raising coconuts, gained their independence in 1977. The population in 1980 numbered about 1,000.** ★★★★

Everyone spoke excellent English at the airfield so there was no communication problem coming in. Getting gas, however, was another story. Gas had to be brought in by truck and arrived in barrels that had to be pumped into the airplane by hand. At eight dollars a gallon, it was quite an expensive stop. Doc had to pay out sixteen hundred dollars for gas. I was appreciating more and more his offer to pay the flying expenses. We left the island just as the sun was setting. Unfortunately, we had not thought to take on extra water in Pago Pago, and the water on Christmas Island was not considered safe to drink, so we had but one twelve-ounce bottle between us to last all the way to Hawaii.

Beautiful Hawaii had its hitches too. We arrived in Honolulu at 2:30 a.m. so the customs people were working overtime. No one seemed to know where the air worthiness registration for the plane was or the bill of sale, so Customs decided to seal the door and wait until the next day. We grabbed our bags and had the hotel pick us up and take us to a Holiday Inn. While the men were registering, I headed for a pay phone and called Delta. There was a flight out at 9:45 the next morning. I was tired, but I didn't want to go to bed and have to get right back up. A quick nap at the airport would be easier so I had the hotel people take me out to the terminal. "Is there anyone around here?" I asked the driver when we got to the airport at Honolulu.

"Sure don't look like it," he said. "Wait. Back there, there's some people." He pointed.

"Oh, good. O.K." I tipped him and went inside before I realized that the people lying on benches with papers over them were street people, not airline customers. I decided to look for another waiting area. A cleaning lady directed me to a coffee shop where I could wait, but I had to sit in the hall while coffee and Coke were handed out a little window.

I arrived in Los Angeles the next day and killed time looking for Ringenbergs in the phone book. I made my next flight to Cincinnati and then home to Fort Wayne in time to attend the bank's Christmas party with Morris. Of course, people wanted to know all about my trip. If it bothers Morris that I get so much attention, he doesn't let on. Sometimes he will ask people if they want to hear about his trip to Cedarville, a little village a few miles from our home. He's joking, I think.

ANOTHER VOICE:

Mary Thompson

My husband and I traveled a lot, all over the world, so I was excited when Margaret Jane told me she was going around the world. I assumed that she and Morris were going on a tour and I was pleased that they were going to see some of the wonderful sights that we had enjoyed. I was actually disappointed when I found out that she was going to fly in a race. To me it didn't seem to be a very enjoyable way to see the world!

When I take a commercial flight, it's kind of neat to sit back and have them bring me coffee, Coke, and peanuts, but I prefer to be the pilot. —Margaret Ringenberg

✈

Weeds in the Garden of Life

I like to compare life to a walk through a garden. My family and friends, as well as my many flying experiences, are the flowers. Every garden, however, has some weeds. In the planning stages of the race around the world, I had encountered a few — concerns about my age, the expense and time involved; but one by one I had plucked and disposed of them. Then suddenly there in my pathway was a giant weed blocking my view of the greatest bouquet of opportunity I could imagine. All communication with Doc stopped. With only a few months to go before the race, he simply stopped calling. Moreover, my calls to him went unanswered. What was wrong?

A month later I knew. He had suffered a

stroke. When he finally called, I could barely understand him. He wanted me to pick up the plane in California, go to Montreal for the required race briefing and then take the plane to Fort Wayne to finish getting it ready. "Maybe we should get a third person just in case," I suggested, but Doc assured me he was still planning to fly the race. Then only a couple of weeks later, he suffered a second stroke. The weeds were sprouting more quickly than I could pull them. I didn't want to drop out of the race. A lot of time and money had been invested. I knew I would not get a second chance, but if I were to fly the race myself, where would I find a copilot on such short notice? One who had the correct license, a passport, visas to all the countries on the race, shots up to date and enough money? Piloting the plane myself, I would need an Australian pilot's license since the plane was registered in Australia.

Much of flying a race is mental. I fly a race in my mind many times before I actually do it. Someone else had been getting the plane ready and I was uncomfortable with that. In my opinion, the plane still needed work. I was still concerned about the gas tanks. Even though there were sufficient tanks to fly long stretches over water, I knew that taking into account the winds and weather conditions, it would be cutting it close to make every leg nonstop over land. I knew I couldn't win with this plane, but I didn't want to quit. It seemed cruel that the whole race idea had been dangled under my nose only to be snatched away at the last moment by circumstances beyond my control.

I called Carolyn Pilaar again. She was will-

ing to go, but only as far as Istanbul. I objected. I
didn't want to start the race if I couldn't finish it.
Time was wasting and I was distraught. I called
another friend. He could meet most of the requirements, but didn't have visas. It was too late to get
them. With only a week to go, I had to face reality.
It was time to quit. I placed a call to the race director in Paris. "Wait," he said, "don't quit yet.
There are two women in Canada who were all set
to fly the race, but the third member of their team
had to withdraw. Please don't quit until you have
talked to them." I called immediately. Adele Fogel
was the owner of a flight school in Toronto. Daphne
Schiff taught the science of flight and meteorology at the University of York. Although neither
had flown a Cessna 340, they were both experienced pilots. Most importantly, they already had
all the necessary papers and money. I had a plane,
but no copilot. They were pilots without a plane.
We knew almost nothing about each other, but the
race was only a week away. If we were not compatible, time would tell. They agreed to fly to Fort
Wayne to meet me and become familiar with the
plane.

The weeds continued to pop up. There were
more problems with the airplane. I discovered that
the exhaust stacks had holes in them. I sent them
to be welded, but the welds didn't hold. It would
cost two thousand dollars to secure reconditioned
ones. I needed another two thousand for a waste
gate. Fortunately, my Canadian copilots agreed
to help with the expense and gas. The plan was
for me to meet them in Montreal for the start of
the race. There had been some last minute changes
in the race route. We were not going to be able to

fly over Saudi Arabia, and the stops at Thailand and Taipei had been changed. I asked Adele and Daphne to redo the maps while I concentrated on the plane. When I arrived in Montreal to find that the maps were not done, I was concerned.

Publicity was swirling around the "hometown" Canadian pilots. I puzzled over the articles in Canadian publications that neglected to mention one important member of the team, the American first pilot. Regardless of what the papers said, I knew I was going to be doing the lion's share of the flying. Neither Adele nor Daphne had flown the Cessna 340 before, so I was unable to add their names to the insurance. While I did not begrudge them their day in the spotlight, I hoped the newspaper coverage was not going to become a problem. I was very serious about completing the race.

Race day was approaching, and I was still pulling weeds. Back in November when we were bringing the airplane back from Australia we had experienced some radio problems. To solve them Doc had all the radios pulled out and replaced with new ones. There hadn't been an opportunity to try out the new radios until I picked up the plane in California and flew it to Fort Wayne to get it ready. As soon as I plugged in my headset overhead, I knew the problem had not been corrected. I immediately unplugged the headset and switched to the hand-held mike. It worked reasonably well, although it did cut out a few times. As soon as I got to Fort Wayne, I asked the radio shop to look at it. They checked it out and assured me it was all taken care of. Then, much to my dismay on the way to Montreal, it happened again. I told Daphne and Adele that using the headsets seemed to foul things up, consequently, we would have to rely on the hand-held mike. They wanted the equipment fixed. At their expense, they had the radio shop look at it. We were assured once again that it was fixed. As we taxied the plane out to start our trip around the world, Daphne and Adele plugged in the headsets. They called the tower — no answer. They called again. Again no answer. Finally the tower said, "If that's Victor Hotel Hotel Mike November (our plane identification VH-HMN) we've got carrier only." Adele and Daphne mistakenly thought that we were on carrier frequency, but the tower simply meant that they knew we were keying the mike, but they could not hear us talking. We tried the hand-held, but this time it didn't work either. Everything had shorted out. We had been third to taxi out, but without clearance there was nothing to do but turn back.

Back in the radio shop, they finally found the problem; frayed wires in the overhead equipment. All it took was a little tape to make them workable, but I was leery. "No one is going to plug in up there," I told my copilots. "Use the hand set."

"But we can't understand the overhead speaker," one insisted. "The headsets are better."

I knew the speaker was difficult to understand at times, but I wasn't taking any chances. "Use the handset," I said. My will prevailed.

✈

On Our Way...At Last

May 1
Legs one and two: Montreal, Quebec, Canada to St. John's,
Newfoundland, Canada to Marrakech, Morocco
(about 3,361 miles)

We got our second start three hours later. Not surprisingly, we were the last to arrive at the refueling stop in St. John's, Newfoundland, just as the fog was rolling in. We gassed up the plane and went to the hotel. Daphne and Adele roomed together, and I was able to share accommodations with a young Spanish racer, Marti Inglada, which reduced my share of the expenses to a mere ten thousand dollars! (Lest this seem like an outrageous amount for room and board, I was to discover that the race organizers spared no expense in obtaining for us the most luxurious accommodations and sumptuous feasts, as well as transportation at each of our stopovers.) She was the youngest contestant at twenty-five

270

while I was the oldest. Sometimes during the duration of the race, she would come in at midnight, and then I would get up at four in the morning, but for the most part we were compatible.

By the next morning the fog had not lifted, and cold temperatures, wind and rain added to the problems. We had breakfast and accepted the box lunches that had been prepared for us. Our drivers had difficulty even seeing the road to the airport. The visibility was so poor we could not see the first planes as they taxied out. By the time it was our turn, the visibility had improved to maybe a half mile. It turned out to be an advantage for me since I disliked flying over water. For two hours, I could see nothing below us but fog. By the time we flew out of it and could see the waves of the Atlantic below us, I was too numb to be nervous. What is that saying about every cloud having a silver lining?

More than six hours later, I spotted mountain peaks coming out of the water. It was an amazing sight! We were coming into the Azores, a group of Portuguese controlled islands about halfway between Newfoundland and Morocco, our next scheduled stop. We refueled there, and it was nearly sundown when we taxied out, but we had to keep going. This race, like the Air Race Classic, was a speed race, but winning did not depend on having the biggest, fastest plane. Each airplane was competing against its optimal speed as determined by the manufacturer, but reality is far from theory. Winds, air traffic control, weather conditions, restricted altitudes and time lost during refueling stops while the stopwatch kept ticking would all play a part. Before we started the race,

I knew that we could not make each leg nonstop without carrying more fuel, but the addition of even two more twenty-gallon tanks would have cost thirteen thousand dollars. The extra stops would cost us the race, but we had no choice. With the addition of a third seat to accommodate our extra crew member, there simply was not enough room for another tank.

Before long, the beautiful blue skies of daylight had turned dark and scary. The unserviceable HF radio did not help matters. We arrived in Morocco in the wee hours of the morning, long after the other racers.

★★★★ **Marrakech, one of the most picturesque cities in Northern Africa, lies in the midst of a palm grove. The old walled city is interesting with its twisting street, markets, tombs and gardens, as well as a sultan's palace. The Kutubiyyah Mosque built in**

1153 boasts a tower 220 feet high. The modern part of the city was built following French occupation in 1913. Population? About 482,000. ★★★★

Our box lunches and the snacks we had picked up in the Azores had been eaten hours earlier. We were famished, but, of course, the dining room was closed at that hour. A surprise, however, awaited me when I got to my room. My roommate was already asleep, but there on the table was a platter of cold meat sandwiches, fruit, cookies and a cold drink. Our organizers had thought of everything.

The next morning we consulted our itinerary. A buffet was to be provided from 7 to 9 a.m., after which we would tour the city. It was a full day of shopping and sightseeing, which included watching snake charmers on the street. Like Dorothy in the Wizard of Oz, I knew I wasn't in Kansas (or Indiana) anymore!

May 5
Leg three: Marrakech, Morocco to Istanbul, Turkey (about 2,132 miles)

We were at the airport bright and early the next morning. We filed our flight plan and then we sat... and sat. Five hours passed between the first takeoff and the last due to heavy air traffic congestion. We wanted to fly at flight level 170, meaning 17,000 feet, but the military was working overhead. When we received clearance to take off two or three hours later, we were instructed to stay below 6,000 feet. Just as I expected, the airplane burned too much fuel at that altitude, and we were compelled to make an extra stop at Tunis for fuel while precious minutes ticked away. It proved to be an interesting, if time-consuming, stop.

We were taken into an open area, since airport officials did not know our purpose for being there. The police came. Customs and emigration officials stood and stared as we exited the plane. "Where's the pilot?" they asked. I shouldn't have been surprised at their confusion; in some countries women aren't even allowed to drive a car. Finally, we were cleared so that we could get fuel. Our hopes of getting under way quickly vanished, however, when they brought us our fuel in barrels! They put a stem into the barrel and we had to crank and crank. When all three of us had exhausted ourselves, some men from the fire station were called on to help us. At least we were not alone in Tunis. Another team had developed a problem with their fuel pump, but had managed to modify it in mid-air. A second team landed complaining of heater problems. They had wrapped their feet in sleeping bags and blankets to keep warm, but their drinking water had frozen. Still another team had lost the use of their autopilot. It was 3 a.m. when we reached Istanbul, Turkey in a dense fog and were cleared for landing . . . with no view of the airport.

★★★★ **Istanbul is the largest city in Turkey. It sits on both sides of the Bosporous Strait that separates Europe from Asia. As a major port, it controls the only passage between the Black Sea and the Mediterranean. It is renowned as one of the most besieged cities in the world, having been assailed by Arabs, Bulgarians and the Fourth Army of the Crusades before falling to the Turks. It was later occupied by Britain, France, and Italy. There are more than 400 mosques, 175 Christian churches and 40 synagogues. Population (1985) was over 5,000, 000.** ★★★★

The next day there was the obligatory press conference and the announcement of leg prizes. Not surprisingly, we were in last place. The unscheduled stop in Tunis had cost us dearly, but it was certainly interesting. Our hotel in Istanbul was located in the center of the old city near the Bazaar, where one can buy or eat anything. We enjoyed our day of sightseeing and a boat tour that took us past historic castles, churches, and the viaducts of ancient Constantinople.

May 7
Leg Four: Istanbul, Turkey to Dubai, United Arab
Emirates (about 1,868 miles)

We were up at 8 o'clock the next morning, but once again, fueling and red-tape delayed our take-off until 11 a.m. It promised to be an interesting flight. Saudi authorities had refused permission for the race to go through their air space, despite the fact that the Saudis held membership in the sponsoring organization, I.C.A.O (International Civil Aviation Organization). As a result, we had been rerouted through Iranian air space. This made the race even more difficult and costly because of the indirect route we had to take to avoid the mountains. Some teams did have to land in Iran to refuel, and, in spite of our perceptions, the people were reported to be friendly and courteous. Race officials had briefed us on what to do if intercepted. If a plane were to come up on our left, drop its wheels and wiggle its wings, we were to follow it and land. We had been instructed to carry veils in the plane in the event of that happening, but I hoped we would not have to use them.

Running low on fuel, we chose Diyarbakir, Turkey, for our next stop because it was a military base and we knew they would have fuel. We had company. Two of our competitors also made a stop there. They knew that one of the planes carrying extra people could not have gotten off the ground back in Istanbul if all its tanks had been filled to capacity. Thus, the extra stop. On the ground, we were met by many people, both American and Turkish, speaking excited English. They didn't get many visitors, I was sure. While we waited, they told us about the American helicopters that had been shot down by our own missiles only two weeks earlier. I could have done just as well without that information. We were interested to learn, however, that we were at the base that was distributing food to the Kurds, victims of the Gulf War.

We refiled our flight plan to get up to flight level 170 and took off. Still caught up in the excitement on the ground, we suddenly realized that a jet was circling to our right. Immediately it swooped under us and then up on the other side. Because it was going so fast we couldn't make out the markings so we had no idea what nationality it was. Holding my breath, I grabbed my camera and snapped a picture just as it sped away. It is indistinguishable in the finished photo, but I know what that little dot is in the lower left corner of the picture. I just don't know who it is! Daphne, who had been using the radio, in spite of warnings that my lower voice would be less likely to attract attention, quickly handed the mike to me. "Here, you do this," she said. After that we were more careful. It was 2 a.m. when we landed in Dubai, totally exhausted.

★★★★ **Dubai is located in an arid region of the Arabian Peninsula bordering the Persian Gulf. It is the chief port and commercial center of the United Arab Emirates. The traditional occupations of pearl diving and fishing have been replaced with oil drilling. Foreign sales of oil and gas financed the creation of a large new city, Jabal Ali. Its population numbers about 419,000.** ★★★★

Even though we were among the last ones to arrive, there was a race committee member

276

there to meet us and help us through customs, a relatively easy task for me, since I had only one bag that weighed eight pounds. Adele and Daphne, on the other hand, required a cart to carry their several suitcases. I was thankful for my WASP training that had taught me to travel light. An oil leak that had to be fixed before we could leave for the hotel 50 kilometers away further delayed us.

We loaded into a cab. I claimed the front seat by virtue of my age. As we traveled, we were told that in the city we could get anything we wanted, cheap, if we haggled. There were no taxes. Despite the fact that it was a Muslim country, we could get alcohol and even bacon for breakfast. All I wanted was a bed. We went through a town and then onto the smoothest blacktop road I had ever seen, but there were no lines on the road and in the darkness it was a bit unnerving. We drove for nearly an hour without seeing anything but sand, and then suddenly there was another blacktop road veering to the right and ahead I could see lights. Before long, the Jebel Ali, a most magnificent hotel, appeared to rise out of the desert. Once we found ourselves inside the walls that surrounded it, the opulence took my breath away. There in the middle of the desert was an oasis of grass and palm trees with a gorgeous swimming pool and spa. The hotel itself was breathtaking with its marble floors.

We enjoyed a welcome respite from the exhaustion of sightseeing the next day. Other than the hotel there was nothing in the desert to see anyway. The pool and spa were wonderfully relaxing. That evening we traveled out into the desert for a barbecue. We marveled at the huge kettles of shrimp, lobster and barbecued meat. The abundance of rice and salads was astounding. Yet, I didn't eat as much as I wanted. We were seated on the floor on cushions at a table barely 18 inches high. Once I got down, it was way too much trouble to get up again, even for a second helping. I relaxed and enjoyed the belly dancers. The high point of my day, however, was opening the Mother's Day card I had brought from home. It said, "And here you go again as an example of how to 'press on to a goal.' I'm very proud of you. I'm glad you're my mom just because of your zest for life. You really are a special person." It was signed by my daughter Marsha. Surrounded by unspeakable wealth, I was reminded of the riches in my life that had nothing to do with money.

May 9
Leg Five: Dubai, UAE to Agra, India (about 1,403 miles)

Leaving Agra, we were told to stick to the airway very precisely. This airway is carefully monitored, and if we tried to "cut corners" we would be intercepted by Indian Mirages and forced to land and explain for hours why we had done it. We were warned that because their VHF radios were not very good, we would have to do a lot of talking and repeating.

There were large crowds at the Agra Air Force Base to welcome us when we landed, including the Indian Minister of State for Petroleum and Natural Gas. Each pilot received a bouquet and a rose garland. The entire road from the airport to the Taj View Hotel was decorated and lined with flags. When we reached the city there was a welcoming committee to greet us, but their hospital-

278

ity was lost on me. I was sick!

★★★★ **Agra is one of the oldest cities on the Indian Peninsula. It is the site of many palaces and mosques including the Taj Mahal which was built by the emperor Shah Jahan as a memorial to his wife. An important trading center, it is famous for handmade gold lace and delicate inlaid mosaics. Population: about 770,000.** ★★★★

Knowing that drinking contaminated water could cause diarrhea, I had been careful to drink only bottled water. How could I have picked up this "bug?" Questioning by the more seasoned world travelers revealed that even the water on my toothbrush could have been the culprit. At any rate, I was not in good shape. The press was there and, naturally, they wanted to talk to the oldest person who was flying around the world. I thought I would never escape. Once in my hotel room, I collapsed on the bed. The much-anticipated trip to the Taj Mahal was out of the question for me. "Don't you at least want to take your shoes off?" my roommate asked, concerned.

"No, I'm too sick," I said.

The next day, consequently, while the others toured the Taj Mahal and ate a splendid lunch, I suffered alone in my room. My roommate was worried and sent a doctor to me. I struggled to the door. "I just need something for diarrhea," I explained. He wanted to come in, but I was so miserable, I shut the door in his face. An hour or so later, two prescriptions, written in a language I couldn't read, were delivered to my door. I noticed a picture of two spoons on the side of one so I took that to mean I should take two spoons full. The other had a picture of a glass and two spoons, so I took two spoons full of that too. I had no idea how often I should take it, but much to my surprise, I not only survived the night but felt much better the next morning, having been treated successfully for my ailment and the resulting dehydration. My friends, who had been able to enjoy the Taj Mahal the day before, paid a price. Many of them had come down with food poisoning following their meal. While I settled for a short visit to a rug factory and a scale model of the Taj Mahal, I tried to view my ordeal of the previous day as another "cloud with a silver lining."

Incidentally, our hotel bill in Agra was over 5,000 rupees. I recovered from the shock once it was translated into American currency: $30.75.

May 11
Leg Six: Agra, India to U'Taphao, Thailand to Ho Chi Minh City, Vietnam (about 2,176 miles)

We departed from Agra the next day without incident, but in the middle of a thunderstorm I had to shoot an approach into the airport at Calcutta for a fuel stop. The employees of Indianoil were quick and courteous, presenting bouquets to each member of the team. They tried to speed us on our way, but it was not to be. Word from the control tower was that airport officials had not been made aware of the race. Flight plans filed the night before at Agra had not reached them; they insisted we file another flight plan and go through Customs and Emigration even though Calcutta was only a technical fueling stop. Which we did, of course. While waiting, they allowed Adele and Daphne to go get us some sandwiches while I stayed with the plane. Then I needed to use the restroom and we were taken to the terminal. Imagine my shock at finding a number of people using the restroom as sleeping quarters. By the time we were cleared for takeoff we had lost three valuable hours to the Indian formalities.

U'Taphao, Thailand, a former U.S. military base, became a compulsory stop for those of us with piston engines. The only gas available in Vietnam was going to be 96-octane Russian fuel, which was incompatible with our Western engines. The race organizers had tried to import fuel for us from Singapore, but the Vietnamese Port Authority refused to allow any ships to be loaded with this "very dangerous product." Attempts to get it by truck from Thailand also failed because the driver didn't want to go through Cambodia. The clock would be stopped for us while in U'Taphao so that we could fill our planes with Avgas 100LL. Then we would fly the 300 nautical miles to Ho Chi Minh City, where we would only top off our tanks with the Russian gas. Since that would constitute just a small quantity and be mixed with the better gas, we all hoped it would not cause trouble with our engines. At least, that was our plan. Moreover, because of the U.S. embargo on Vietnam, it would be nearly impossible to get small parts.

But, if Calcutta had been a bad dream, U'Taphao was a nightmare. As each team arrived, we discovered that we could not refuel and take off. Pilots, sick and dehydrated, collapsed under their planes, trying to regain enough strength to go on. At first, authorities denied knowledge of the race at all. Then an officer of the oil company arrived and, while he admitted that he knew about the race, he explained that he did not have adequate Avgas for us all. He had calculated what he thought our small planes would need and, feeling that our demand was excessive, he had obtained a smaller quantity. The company had allotted a certain amount of fuel and he was not authorized to give us more. Fueling was slow, about an hour per plane. By 11 p.m. with only two planes to go, including ours, they ran out of gas. The linemen could not get more fuel for us without the commander's orders, and he was home asleep. They would not call him until morning. A little while later one of the Bonanzas came back after running into a thunderstorm. So there we were, three teams with nothing to do but wait. We could not leave the base to get anything to eat because we had not yet been cleared by Customs, and due to the nature of the maneuvers that were taking place there, the base commander seemed very wary of us. We scrounged chips and snacks at the PX.

Adele was still not feeling up to par after her bout with food poisoning and we were all tired. We tried to snatch some sleep on the only seats available, but the lights were too bright and we could not convince anyone to turn them off. At about 3 a.m. one of the guards took pity on us and said that he would take responsibility if we wanted to go down the street to a hotel. We loaded our gear into the back of an old pickup truck and someone took us to the hotel. Once there we were thankful for the beds, but the atmosphere wasn't exactly conducive to sleep. A dog tied to a pillar in the lobby barked continuously while we were trying

to check in. Every few minutes the clerk would go
over and kick the dog and tell him to "shut up."
We were given rooms at the top of the stairs and
that dog barked all night. In the morning we hurried back to the airport for a breakfast of potato
chips and another delay. Finally at noon we got
our gas and headed for Vietnam. We arrived in
Ho Chi Minh City exhausted and hungry at 6 p.m.
on Friday the 13th.

★★★★ **Ho Chi Minh City, formerly Saigon, is
located on the Saigon River near the Mekong Delta.
It is the country's largest city. The scene of heavy
fighting during the Vietnam war, the population grew
rapidly as refugees settled there. When the war ended
in 1975, it was captured by the North Vietnamese and
the name was changed to Ho Chi Minh City,
population about 4,000,000.** ★★★★

I was disappointed to learn that we could
not all stay at the same hotel. Adele and Daphne
were dropped at one hotel and I was taken to another. The lobby of my hotel was beautiful, with a
giant chandelier and lots of glass. When I asked
for my key, I was told that my roommate had been
given the only key. I grabbed my suitcase and got
on the elevator. The ordinary-looking elevator did
not prepare me for the paint-splattered cement
walls of the hallway leading to my room. I started
down the hall, realized I was going the wrong way,
and backtracked until I found our room at the opposite end. I knocked. Marti wasn't there. I was
exhausted, having been up most of the previous
night. Reminiscent of my WASP days, I dropped
my bag, sat down and tried to take a nap in a hallway that looked like a good setting for a murder. I

was too tired to care. Soon one of the hotel workers spotted me and asked, "Are you all right?"

"No!" I said. "I can't get into my room."

"I'll get you some help, "she said.

Before long, someone came with a key and let me in. "The meeting for your group is downstairs," she told me. I hadn't even thought to look at my itinerary. Suddenly I was thankful for having been brought to this hotel. The others would have to walk from their hotel to ours for dinner. It was all I could do to walk to the dining room. I heard later that street gangs had attacked some of the race participants, snatching their valuables. One man who had to pay $25 to recover his stolen passport, barely escaped the youths who converged on him in the narrow hotel hallway.

For the most part, though, I found the Vietnamese to be open and friendly. I was surprised that even after two lengthy wars, they seemed to hold no ill will toward either the Americans or the French, and they were anxious to show off their Eastern hospitality. We were taken on a bus, amidst throngs of motorbikes, to a location where we boarded a boat for a trip through the Mekong Delta. The weather was hot and humid and the scenery beautiful with flowers everywhere. I found the rice paddies interesting, and the Vietnamese were proud to point out that their rice is exported to the United States. We marveled at the little iron fences enclosing tombstones in the midst of the rice fields and were told that if field workers died, their families simply buried them there. Up river we were able to walk around a village where we were offered an abundance of fruit to eat. We had been warned to choose fruits like bananas because it was not safe to eat anything with the skin on even if it was washed. Especially if it had been washed, I thought, recalling my experience with the water in India. I was told we could sample snake or rat for lunch, but I stuck to the fruit.

ANOTHER VOICE:

Patricia Jayne Keefer

We were in Vietnam, about as far from home as we could get, during the 1994 world race, when Mom became very ill and was unable to fly the next leg to Japan. Margaret was flying an unfamiliar aircraft with two inexperienced pilots so she had her own challenges in this 24-day race around the world, but she had managed to stay calm and keep smiling. We were all excrutiatingly tired by that time, but Margaret had enough strength to take care of her responsibilities and still watch out for others.

I had taken over the pilot-in-command responsibilities as well as the copilot duties for our plane. When I set about refueling on the steamy ramp in Vietnam, I realized the Vietnamese fuel nozzle was too large to fit in the 72 gallon auxiliary tank we had mounted inside the fuselage. Seeing my dilemma, Margaret came to the rescue with a cutoff plastic oil container that acted as a funnel. It was a seemingly small act of kindness, but to me it spoke volumes about her as a person. Not only did she notice the problem, she came forward, without being asked, with a solution for a competitor. It is incidents such as this that change flying friendships into family relationships.

May 14
Leg Seven: Ho Chi Minh City to Naha, Okinawa, Japan
(about 1,730 miles)

The takeoff from Ho Chi Minh City was erratic. Bangkok suddenly decided to close its air space to the race after some aircraft were airborne, and those planes were made to return from the takeoff point to refile flight plans. Our next stop was to have been Taipei, but Taiwan had refused us entry for political reasons. It seems that the French president had made some sort of deal with Communist China, and now Taiwan would have nothing to do with the French-affiliated race. Consequently, we went to Okinawa, but not before another ill-fated fuel stop in Manila, where they tried to take advantage of us by charging a $350 landing fee. Perhaps they thought female pilots wouldn't know the difference. The Okinawans, still reveling in their "liberation" from the U.S., rankled the veterans among us, but our hotel was beautiful with balconies facing the beach. We were able to relax and had time to do some laundry, which seemed like quite a luxury.

★★★★ **Okinawa is an island off southwest Japan It consists of flat, sloping beds of volcanic ash over older rock. The climate is hot and humid and typhoons frequently strike in the summer. Until the 19th century it was an independent country, but later paid tribute to China and then Japan. U.S. forces landed on the island during World War II, and it became the site of bitter fighting. Okinawa remained under U.S. control until 1972, when it was returned to Japan. The population in 1985 was about 1,000,000.** ★★★★

May 17

Leg Eight: Naha, Okinawa, Japan, to Sendai, Japan
(about 1,129 miles)

Going into Sendai the next day, we were told to stick to official aeronautical phraseology. "Don't try to tell a joke to the controllers," our organizers said. I wondered why anyone would. Our daylight flight took us past Hiroshima and Nagasaki, a sobering experience. We landed on a short strip on the seashore that wasn't visible until the last moment. Daphne likened it to "landing a Zero on an aircraft carrier." Everyone commented on the number of golf courses visible from the air. We had looked forward to the view of Mount Fuji, but were a bit disappointed when it was shrouded in clouds. The weather was fabulous with great tailwinds coming into Sendai, and what's more, just for that leg we had moved up to fourth place!

★★★★ **Sendai is the largest city in northern Japan, located on Honshu Island. It is sometimes called the "forest capital" because of its many groves and surrounding wooded hills. It is a principal trading center for salt and fish. Of interest in the city are a 17th century castle, horticultural gardens and a shrine that is designated a national treasure. Population? About 865,000.** ★★★★

There was great press reception and, as usual, they were interested in the three "grandma" fliers. Later, in the hotel, I got a kick out of watching myself be interviewed on TV. Everything in Sendai was very expensive. We had the oil changed and oil filter replaced although maintenance fees were ninety dollars an hour and gas six dollars a

287

gallon. The streets were full of kiosks selling turtles of all sizes for soup. I couldn't ask what those cost since very few people spoke English.

May 19
Leg Nine: Sendai, Japan, to Petropavlovsk,
Siberia (about 1,478 miles)

Leaving Sendai was a problem for us. We wanted to go north, but Air Traffic Control had us turn out and go south for 20 to 30 minutes and then climb to 17,000 feet before turning back. The Japanese would not allow us to go over their military installations except at a certain altitude. So forty-five minutes later we were right back where we started. Forty-five minutes had been our reserve to get to Russia and I knew I did not have enough fuel left. My extra stops along the way had not been planned, but I had gotten information from the Aircraft Owners and Pilots Association (A.O.P.A.) and the race officials on where 100-octane fuel could be obtained and had highlighted all the spots on my map with a marker. I radioed ahead to Sapporo, Japan, to see if they had gas. They did, but when we got on the ground, there was a big discussion about whether they could sell it to us. We were told that Japan does not export gas to Russia. Indeed, they questioned whether they could even gas up a plane that was going to Russia. Never mind the technicality that we were going to burn the gas on the way, not deliver it to Russia. We finally came to an agreement, but it had wasted a lot of time.

Up to this point we had not had any problems with the airplane, but after leaving Sapporo we noticed that the connections for the gas tanks inside the plane were dripping gas on the floor, and the cockpit was filled with fumes. As we climbed, it started to get cold, but we were afraid to turn on the heater for fear of sparks. Before reaching Russia we decided we would have to risk it to keep from freezing. We didn't explode.

The time was getting on toward 11 p.m. as we approached Russia. It was still daylight and we could see the mountain peaks ahead, but the valley was filled with fog. We radioed the airport, asking for information. What was the ceiling and visibility? The answer in Russian-accented English was in meters. I didn't understand. There was no radar or air traffic control. We did not have enough gas to get back to Japan and there was no place else to get gas, so we had no choice but to shoot the approach. I may have appeared calm, but seriously I did not know if we could get in or not. It was reported later that due to the lack of navigational aids, some of the planes had come perilously close to the volcanoes in Kamchatka Plateau. I had no desire to know if one of them was mine.

★★★★ **Petropavlovsk is the capital and chief port of the Kamchatka region of Siberia. Located on the southeast coast of Kamchatka Peninsula, it lies in a narrow valley between forested mountains. The harbor is ice-blocked from November to May.** ★★★★

It was cold in Russia — 2 degrees at night — and the snow was piled two feet high in places. We have some unpredictable weather in Indiana, but I had never thought of May as a winter month. The Russians were efficient with a mobile Immigration and Customs office in a coach that moved from aircraft to aircraft. They cleared everyone within minutes of landing. The vice-mayor of the city was there to greet us. The city and airport had recently been opened to international air traffic, and they were looking forward to receiving their first tourists that summer. But, to us there was a closed-in look about it. One of the race committee members rode with us to the hotel and on the way he tried to paint a glowing picture of Kamchatka Spa, where we would be staying. He described the red-carpeted hallways and the swimming pool, but something told me it wouldn't exactly be the Ritz. My suspicions were confirmed when we pulled up in front of a cement block building — our hotel.

We did not have to register, but rather open a small sliding door and reach in for the key. Everybody else's key was in there too. When checking out, a patron would simply drop the key back in. Everybody had access to the keys, so I wondered why we even bothered locking our rooms. We went into a little hallway and there were two rooms, each with two metal cots. To the left there was a bathroom with a porcelain stool minus the seat. On the floor next to it was a wooden ring which had to be placed on the toilet when needed. The pipes were rusted. I was right; it wasn't the Ritz.

May 21

Leg 9: Petropavlovsk, Siberia to Anchorage, Alaska (about 2,019 miles)

Our next stop was Nome, Alaska. It had just recently been made a port of entry, yet when we arrived, there was no one there who could see us through Customs. The man who sold us our gas said, "I'll just go ahead and give you the gas.

Then you can go to Anchorage and enter the U.S. there." We had left Petropavlovsk on May 21 and arrived in Anchorage at a late hour on May 20! That International Dateline business again.

★★★★ **Anchorage is Alaska's largest city and main center of commerce and transportation. It was founded in 1914 as a construction camp for the railroad and became the headquarters for the Alaska Defense Command during WWII. It was severely damaged in a 1964 earthquake. It appears that the whole city is involved in aviation. There are 10,000 airplanes in the city. Population about 226,000.** ★★★★

There are three major and two minor airfields serving Anchorage, all within a radius of ten miles with roads crossing runways and runways crossing roads. We could see aircraft taking off and landing from all directions, including those taking off and landing on the lakes with floats.

Ironically, Customs at Anchorage was the most difficult we had encountered. We had to wait inside the airplane for over an hour for the Customs and Immigration staff to arrive and let us out. When they did, they caught the fact that I did not have the registration for the plane. After some discussion, it was decided that since the bill of sale from Australia stated that it was good until the registration arrived and did not specify a definite time, it was valid. Imagine, I had gone all the way around the world on a bill of sale, and no one noticed until I got back to the U.S! In spite of these minor inconveniences, I did not complain. The United States was still the greatest place in the world to me. In some countries we had to pay to use their air space, and landing fees in some places were as much as six hundred dollars with gas eight dollars a gallon!

May 22
Leg Eleven: Anchorage, Alaska, to Calgary, Alberta, Canada (about 1,517 miles)

Obtaining fuel at Anchorage had been much like driving into a gas station. The aircraft taxied in, filled up, and lined up for takeoff. Due to the staggered takeoffs, our arrivals at Calgary stretched from mid-day to late night.

★★★★ **Calgary, the largest city in Alberta Province, was established in 1875 as an outpost of the Northwest Mounted Police. It is rich in oil and coal. More than 300 oil companies have main offices here. It is the home of the nation's largest zoo and the site of one of the most famous rodeos, the Annual Calgary Exhibition and Stampede. Population (1986) 636,000.** ★★★★

The reception at Calgary surpassed all previous receptions when a red carpet was rolled out at the steps of each arriving aircraft! On hand to greet us were the Mounties and a female sheriff complete with guns and handcuffs. In true western tradition, each of us was "branded" on the back of the hand. We were then treated to a wonderful Western-style barbecue with huge steaks, a welcome change from the exotic food of previous days. While some of the race participants went horseback riding, I did not. Visiting the site of the Calgary Olympics was a real treat, but the closer we got to home, the more anxious I was to keep going.

May 25
Leg Twelve: Calgary, Alberta, Canada to Montreal,
Quebec, Canada (about 1,850 miles)

We arrived back in Montreal having traveled over 15,000 miles. As we taxied up to the Aerotaxi parking bays at St. Hulbert Airfield, the same field from which we had begun our adventure, we were greeted by thunderous applause. Dozens of well-wishers had turned out with banners, bouquets, and champagne to welcome all of us home. I watched the emotional reunions of friends and families with a sense of sadness, knowing that mine would have to wait until my return to Fort Wayne. The media, too, had turned out in large numbers, seeking interviews and reactions from the racers. Adele and Daphne offered to go out and unload the plane. "Wait, I'll help you," I said, catching up. I wasn't going to let anyone unload the airplane and my stuff without me.

"Oh, no, you don't need to," they assured me. I insisted. We had a slight disagreement over who would keep the umbrella that had been given to the team.

"That stays with the airplane," I said.

"Why?"

"It just does," I said. I got busy unloading, and when I walked around the plane, my two copilots were talking to a reporter. I understood then why they had not wanted me to help them. They had scheduled an interview with the Canadian press and didn't want me to interfere. I shrugged it off. I knew what I had accomplished. The media were just not important to me at that time.

Vijaypat Singhania, the race pilot from India, invited us all to a party on him that night. He provided a wonderful dinner and flowers for all of us. I didn't think that money was an object, since he had taken two airplanes around the world — one that he flew and the other to carry his gear, a spare pilot, and extra parts. A large delegation of his family and friends had flown in from India to greet him. The next day at the awards ceremony, he was pronounced the winner of Group III — Turbo Prop Division. There was no trophy, no cash prize, just the feeling of satisfaction, a glass of champagne and, of course, bragging rights. When the scores were tallied, we had placed last in our group, but as one of my teammates said, ". . . winning was so unimportant to everyone. Everybody who raced and made it home safely is a winner."

I certainly felt like a winner when I arrived in Fort Wayne to a cheering crowd of family and friends even though I had been delayed two hours by weather and Customs problems reentering the United States. A brass band made up of my daughter and grandchildren greeted me with "Back Home Again in Indiana" as I got out of the plane. The red carpet was rolled out just for me by members of the Three Rivers Ninety-Nines. And there was Morris with a single red rose! I felt as though I could live on that moment alone for a long time. But . . . my granddaughter was performing in a Christian dance recital that night and Grandma just had to be there. And the Air Race Classic was coming up in a few weeks and. . .

"There were no losers in this race. It took a lot of courage, strength and talent (just to finish)."-Vijaypat Singhania

Below is a time sheet from the around the world race indicating the hours each pilot flew the plane. L, meaning left seat, designates the pilot in command.

	Ringenberg	Schiff	Fogel
	L	L	L
St. Hubert's/St. John's	3.7		
St. John's/Azores	6.5		
Azores/Marrakech	4.5		
Marrakech/Tunis	5.0		
Tunis/Istanbul	5.0		
Istanbul/Diyarbakir	3.4		
Diyarbakir/Dubai	6.8		
Dubai/Agra	6.5		
Agra/Calcutta			3.7
Calcutta/Utaphao		6.2	
Utaphao/Ho Chi Minh	3.5		
Ho Chi Minh/Manila	5.0		
Manila/Okinawa			4.9
Okinawa/Sendai		5.9	
Sendai/Sapporo	2.5		
Sapporo/Petropavlovsk	5.6		
Petropavlovsk/Nome	7.1		
Nome/Anchorage	3.1		
Anchorage/Whitehorse			3.2
Whitehorse/Calgary		5.1	
Calgary/North Bay	6.7		
North Bay/Montreal	1.8		
Left seat totals	76.7	17.2	11.8

ANOTHER VOICE:

Steve Wright

When the drivers at T.N.T. Holland where I worked heard that the local woman who was flying around the world was my mother-in-law, they asked me for daily reports. I was amazed at how many people were interested in her adventure. I think I hadn't appreciated the magnitude of her accomplishments until the night I sat in the Embassy Theater and watched her being honored with other "celebrities" in the Bicentennial Salute to the Stars. She was in great company with Sweet Louis, Hilliard Gates, and Shelly Long. I was so proud when she made her brief speech. I enjoyed being her son-in-law immensely that night. During the time she was flying around the world, Marsha entered and won third place in an essay contest sponsored by Target and Ladies' Home Journal. The topic was "My mother is one smart lady because. . ." She had good material to work with.

Lois Feigenbaum

When Margaret flew the around the world race in 1994, she was very "iffy" about making the flight. She wanted me to go along since I had many hours in a plane similar to the type she would be flying. The price was more than I wanted to spend, but I told her to go ahead as this was the trip of a lifetime. GO! Not only did she complete the race, but on her return, she became quite a celebrity, and was asked to make many speaking appearances. She was more afraid of the public speaking than she was of the flight. With some encouragement from me and others, she now speaks everywhere, and not only on her Around the World Flight, but on air racing in general or any other subject she knows. She has lost her shyness and holds her own under any circumstance. She is a delight to be with.

Margaret was inducted into the Forest of Friendship in 1994 and certainly epitomizes the slogan of the Forest—"World Friendship Through Flying." I was there the day she was inducted. It was certainly a happy day for Margaret and I was proud to be there.

And So On. . .

Looking back on the race around the world and thinking about flying over the water, all the planning, the strangeness of foreign cultures, I realize what an accomplishment it was for me personally. Would I do it again? Yes, but next time it will be in a jet because of the trouble getting aviation gas at the different landing sites around the globe. There were discomforts, to be sure, warm bottled water, ice, fog, thunderstorms, dust storms, illness. Sometimes it was too hot. Other times it was too cold. But for every discomfort, there were dozens of wonderful things — new sights, new places, new things to learn, interesting people. Since I have returned I have ridden in parades, made the front page of the *Indianapolis*

Star, and the back page of the *National Enquirer.* I have been named a "Fort Wayne Super Star," and have flown left seat in a restored B-24. I have been featured on a PBS show and interviewed for German television. And, I have given speeches, dozens of speeches, including one to a thousand cadets at the Air Force Academy in Colorado Springs. At first, I thought of the public speaking as one of those "weeds" in my life, but now I am enjoying it immensely as a new aspect of my flying career. What a wonder that all these good things have come to me just because I got to do what I love to do most — fly. If my dad were still alive, I think he would be proud that I took his advice to heart: "You can do whatever you put your mind to."

"Though the course you're on may change headings along the way, just remember -- the sky's the limit, your future's bright, and it's not where you've come from, but where you are going that counts. Aim high!" -- Margaret Ringenberg, in a speech to Air Force Academy Cadets, 1998

A. List of Abbreviations

AAF-	Army Air Force
AAFFTD-	Army Air Force Flying Training Detachment
A.O.P.A.-	Aircraft Owners and Pilots Association
ARC-	Air Race Classic
AT-	Advanced trainer
ATC-	Air Transport Command, also Air Traffic Control
AVGAS-	Aviation gas
AWTAR-	All Woman Transcontinental Air Race
B-	Designation for bomber planes
BOQ-	Bachelor Officer Quarters
BT-	Basic trainer
CAA-	Civil Aeronautics Authority
CAP-	Civil Air Patrol
CPT-	Civilian Pilot Training
E-ride-	Elimination ride
FAA-	Federal Aviation Authority
F.A.I.R.-	Fairladies' Annual Indiana air Race
FBO-	Fixed Base Operator
GPS-	Global Positioning System
HF-	High frequency
HQ-	Headquarters
IFR-	Instrument Flight Rules
ILS-	Instrument landing system
LAX-	Los Angeles Airport
NCAAB-	New Castle Army Air Base
ONC-	Operational Navigation Chart
P-	Designation for pursuit or fighter planes such as P-51
PT-	Primary Trainer

RON-	Remain Overnight
R & R	Rest and Recreation leave
S.M.A.L.L.	Southern Michigan All Lady lark
VFR-	Visual Flight Rules
VHF-	Very High Frequency
VOR-	Very high frequency Omnidirectional Radio range
WAC-	Women's Army Corps
WAFS-	Women's Auxiliary Flying Squadron
WASP-	Women Airforce Service Pilots
WFTD-	Women's Flying Training Detachment

B. Races in which Margaret has flown

Americana Grand Prix Air Race
Angel Derby International Air Race
Air Race Classic
Bahamas Grand Prix Air Race
Great Southern Air Race
Indiana F.A.I.R.
Indiana Grand Prix
Illi-nines Air Derby
Kentucky Air Derby
Michigan S.M.A.L.L.
Petticoat Air Derby
Powder Puff Derby (AWTAR)
Shangri-La Grand Prix
Shoreline Drag
Three River's Derby

C. Planes that Margaret has Flown

Military

Beechcraft	C-45, (AT-11), (AT-7) 450(UC-45) Kansan Bombadier, gunner trainer, 450 hp
Cessna	UC-78 (AT-17) Bobcat, Bamboo Bomber Adv. trainer, cargo, 245 hp
Consolidated	B-24 Liberator (As copilot) Heavy bomber, 1200 hp
Douglas	C-47 (DC-3) Dakota Transport, 1200 hp C-54 Skymaster (As copilot) cargo, 1350 hp
Fairchild	PT-19, PT-19A, PT-19B (PT-26) Trainer, 175 hp
Lockheed	C-56E Lodestar Transport, 1200 hp
North American	AT-6 (AT-16) (BC-1) Texan Adv. trainer, 600 hp
Piper	L-4 Grasshopper, Cub Glider tow, cargo, 65 hp C-78
Taylorcraft	L-2 Grasshopper Glider tow, cargo, 65hp
Vultee	BT-13 Basic Trainer, 450 hp

Non-military planes

Beechcraft	Bonanza, Bonanza S-35, Bonanza K-35, Bonanza J-35, Bonanza E-35, 225-285 hp
Beechcraft	Baron
Beechcraft	Musketeer, 160 hp
Bellanca	Super Viking, 290 hp
Cessna	340
Cessna	R172-K, 195 hp
Cessna	Skylane 182-N, 230 hp
Cessna	172, 145 hp
Champion	C-90-12F, 90 hp
Mooney	Ranger, M20C, M20G, and other models, 180 hp
Mooney	A2-A Cadet
Piper	P28-160, 140, 180, 160 hp
Piper	J-3, J-4, J-5 Cub, 65 hp
Piper	Lance, 300 hp
Piper	PA-24, 400 hp
Piper	Cherokee

Air Race Classic. . .Reflections 1977-1986, compiled
        by H. Glenn Buffington, San Diego,
        California, 1986.

Churchill, Jan, On wings to War: Teresa James,
        Aviator, Sunflower University Press,
        Manhattan, Kansas, 1992.

Cochran, Jacqueline and Maryann Bucknum
        Brinley, The Autobiography of the Greatest
        Woman Pilot in Aviation History, Bantam,
        Toronto, 1987.

Cole, Jean Hascall, Women Pilots of World War II,
        University of Utah Press, Salt Lake
        City, 1992.

"Girl Pilots," Life, July 19, 1943, pp. 73-81.

"Grabill Flyers Speed Home from Spokane, Wash. after
        Transcontinental Race, Suburban Life, July 16,
        1959

Granger, Byrd Howell, On Final Approach: The
        Women Airforce Service Pilots of World
        War II, Falconer Publishing Co., Scottsdale,
        Arizona, 1991.

Keil, Sally Van Wagenen, Those Wonderful Women in
        Their Flying Machines: The Unknown Heroines
        of World War II, Rawson Wade Publishers, Inc.,
        New York, 1979.

Miller, Curt, "Margaret Ringenberg: Racing With the
        Wind," Business People, September 1991, pp. 5-
        10.

Moolman, Valerie and the Editors of Time Life
        Books, Women Aloft, Time Life Books,   Al-
        exandria, Virginia, 1981.

Powder Puff Derby: The Record, 1947-1977, All-Woman Transcontinental Air Race, Inc.,1985.

Round the World Air Race '94, (video tape.)

Scharr, Adele Riek, _Sisters in the Sky, Vol.II, The WASP_, The Patrice Press, St. Louis, 1988.

Selby, Barbara, "The Fifinellas," _Flying_, July 1943.

Taylor, Frank J. , "Our Women Warriors," _Liberty_, January 29, 1944, pp.26-28.

Verges, Marianne, _On Silver Wings: The Women Airforce Service Pilots of World War II 1942-1944_, Ballantine Books, New York, 1991.

Weaver, Kay and Martha Wheelock, _One Fine Day_, Circe Records and Ishtar Films.

Whyte, Edna Gardner with Ann L. Cooper, _Rising Above It_, Orion Books, New York, 1991.

Women of Courage: The Story of the Women Pilots of World War II, K.M. Productions, Inc., Lakewood, Colorado.

Wood, Winifred, _We Were Wasps_, (self-published), 1978.

Order Form

✉ For each book send check or money order to:

Daedalus Press
P.O. Box 8962
Fort Wayne, IN 46898-8962
Tel: (219) 484-4731

❑ Please send ___copies of "Girls Can't Be Pilots"
to:

Name:_____

Address:_____

City: _____ State: _____

Zip: _____-_____

Telephone: (_____) _____

Price: $14.95 per book. Indiana residents
please add 5%

Shipping and handling: $3.00 for up to 3 books to
the same address.